Governing Interorganizational Relationships for Innovation

Stefano Li Pira · Anna Moretti

Governing Interorganizational Relationships for Innovation

The Case of the Italian Automotive Industry

Stefano Li Pira
Warwick Business School
University of Warwick
Coventry, UK

Anna Moretti
Venice School of Management
Università Ca' Foscari Venezia
Venezia, Venezia, Italy

ISBN 978-3-031-50228-6   ISBN 978-3-031-50229-3 (eBook)
https://doi.org/10.1007/978-3-031-50229-3

© The Editor(s) (if applicable) and The Author(s), under exclusive license to Springer Nature Switzerland AG 2024

This work is subject to copyright. All rights are solely and exclusively licensed by the Publisher, whether the whole or part of the material is concerned, specifically the rights of translation, reprinting, reuse of illustrations, recitation, broadcasting, reproduction on microfilms or in any other physical way, and transmission or information storage and retrieval, electronic adaptation, computer software, or by similar or dissimilar methodology now known or hereafter developed.
The use of general descriptive names, registered names, trademarks, service marks, etc. in this publication does not imply, even in the absence of a specific statement, that such names are exempt from the relevant protective laws and regulations and therefore free for general use.
The publisher, the authors, and the editors are safe to assume that the advice and information in this book are believed to be true and accurate at the date of publication. Neither the publisher nor the authors or the editors give a warranty, expressed or implied, with respect to the material contained herein or for any errors or omissions that may have been made. The publisher remains neutral with regard to jurisdictional claims in published maps and institutional affiliations.

Cover illustration: © Melisa Hasan

This Palgrave Macmillan imprint is published by the registered company Springer Nature Switzerland AG
The registered company address is: Gewerbestrasse 11, 6330 Cham, Switzerland

Paper in this product is recyclable.

Contents

1 **Introduction**   1
   1.1 Governance Mechanisms and the Impact of Disruption on Interorganizational Relationships   2
   1.2 Exploring the Landscape: Unravelling the Typology of Governance Mechanisms in Interorganizational Relationships   3
   1.3 Disruption in Inter-organizational Relationships   6
   1.4 Exploring the Transformation of the Automotive Industry: A Methodological Clarification   11
   1.5 Overview of the Book   13
   References   14

2 **Exchange Hazards and Governance Choices**   19
   2.1 Contractual and Relational Governance and Exchange Hazards   20
   2.2 Governing Collaborations at the Dyad Level   21
      2.2.1 Partners' Features and Exchange Hazards   21
      2.2.2 Relationship's Features and Exchange Hazards   24
   2.3 Governing Collaborations at the Portfolio Level   27
      2.3.1 Exchange Hazards at the Portfolio Level   28
      2.3.2 Exchange Hazards at the Focal-Firm Level from a Portfolio Perspective   29
   2.4 Governing Collaborations at the Whole Network Level   30
      2.4.1 Exchange Hazards at the Network Level   31

		2.4.2	Exchange Hazards at the Focal-Firm Level from a Network Perspective	34
	2.5		Concluding Remarks: The Contingent Value of Governance Mechanisms	36
	References			37

3 Dynamics of Governance Mechanisms in Interorganizational Relationships ... 49
  3.1 Introduction ... 50
  3.2 Evolution and Adaptation of Governance Mechanisms in Response to Shifting Interorganizational Relationships Under Disruption ... 52
    3.2.1 Problem Solving Approach to Governance of IORs ... 52
    3.2.2 Experiential Learning Approach to Governance of IORs ... 54
    3.2.3 Evolutionary Approach to Governance of IORs ... 56
    3.2.4 Political Approach to Governance of IORs ... 57
  3.3 Governance Mechanism's Replication ... 59
    3.3.1 Defining Replication Strategies ... 60
    3.3.2 Unravelling the Replication of Governance Forms Through a Multi-perspective Analysis ... 61
  3.4 Conclusion ... 65
  References ... 66

4 Collaborative Innovation in the Italian Automotive Supply-Chain ... 71
  4.1 Innovation in the Automotive Industry ... 72
  4.2 Innovating in the Italian Automotive Industry ... 74
  4.3 The EVs Transition of the Automotive Industry ... 76
  4.4 The Case of the Italian Automotive Supply-Chain: Governance Choices and Innovation ... 78
  4.5 Exchange Hazards and the Choice of Governance Mechanisms ... 80
    4.5.1 The Dyadic Level of Analysis ... 81
    4.5.2 The Portfolio Level of Analysis ... 83
    4.5.3 The Network Level of Analysis ... 85
  4.6 The Diffusion of Governance Choices ... 86
  4.7 Governance Choices and Firms' Performance ... 89
  4.8 Concluding Remarks ... 92
  References ... 93

5	Governing IORs for Innovation in Times of Disruption	97
	5.1 The Challenges of Governing IORs for Innovation in Times of Disruption	98
	5.2 How Firms Mitigate the Risks of Inter-organizational Relationships? The Contingent Value of Governance Mechanisms	100
	5.3 How Firms Develop Their Governance Strategies? A Complex Organizational Capability	101
	5.4 Concluding Remarks and Future Directions	104
	References	106

Index   109

List of Tables

Table 4.1 Partners' and relationships' features and governance choices 81
Table 4.2 Portfolio's features and governance choices 84
Table 4.3 Focal-firm's features at the network level and governance choices 86
Table 4.4 The diffusion of governance choice at the portfolio and network level 87
Table 4.5 The performance effects of governance choices 91

CHAPTER 1

Introduction

Abstract The realm of interorganizational relationships and their influence on firms' innovation have garnered significant attention, underscoring the crucial role of governance mechanisms in determining firm success. Performance disparities among firms engaged in IORs have become evident, with some effectively managing these partnerships while others struggle with high failure rates. The rise of technological disruption has emerged as a formidable force impacting the value of such relationships. The chapter explores the dynamics of governance mechanisms and their interplay with disruption, with a particular focus on the rapidly evolving automotive industry undergoing a transition to electric vehicles. By examining various forms of governance and their implications within this context, we seek to enhance understanding of how firms can effectively govern IORs in the face of disruption. This research contributes to filling the existing gap in the literature regarding the relationship between governance mechanisms, disruption, and firm performance in the realm of IORs.

Keywords Interorganizational relationships · Governance mechanisms · Technological disruption · Automotive industry · Electric vehicles

© The Author(s), under exclusive license to Springer Nature Switzerland AG 2024
S. Li Pira and A. Moretti, *Governing Interorganizational Relationships for Innovation*,
https://doi.org/10.1007/978-3-031-50229-3_1

1.1 Governance Mechanisms and the Impact of Disruption on Interorganizational Relationships

The realm of interorganizational relationships (IORs) and their impact on firms' innovative output has been widely acknowledged, highlighting the pivotal role of governance mechanisms in determining firm success (Zollo et al., 2002). As more firms recognize the specific advantages of engaging in IORs, it becomes evident that there are notable performance disparities among them, with some effectively undertaking these partnerships while others struggling with high failure rates. Although several theoretical perspectives have generated mixed and inconclusive findings (Cao et al., 2013; Keller et al., 2021), the question of how firms define effective IOR governance strategies remains partially unanswered.

In today's ever-changing business landscape, the significance of performance disparities between firms that actively participate in interorganizational relationships and those that neglect such engagements cannot be underestimated. Technological disruption has emerged as a formidable force capable of significantly impacting the value of these relationships. In the field of management, the language of disruption has been consistently used to explore the emergence, evolution, and transformation of industry ecosystems. Within these ecosystems, the success of firms relies on the coordination and strategic alignment not only with traditional suppliers but also with other ecosystem members who function as "complementors" (Brandenburger & Nalebuff, 1997). The existing literature has primarily concentrated on the ways in which IORs can assist firms during periods of disruption. For instance, Ansari et al. (2016) study exemplified how alliances can be utilized to disrupt established ecosystems. Kapoor and Lee (2013) research uncovered that alliances play a pivotal role in fostering trust within an industry. Additionally, Furr and Shipilov (2018) work provided insights into the construction of new ecosystems through the formation of alliances.

Past literature on IORs has highlighted the significance of governance in determining their successful outcomes. Understanding how to effectively govern IORs is crucial for aligning them with a changing competitive landscape.

The longstanding debate originating from transaction cost economics, as proposed by Williamson (1979), has discussed the management of IORs through formal or informal mechanisms, or a combination of both.

To assess the value of these mechanisms, previous studies have examined firms' utilization of formal contracts and other tangible documents that serve as evidence of partners' formal agreements. Examples of such documents include business plans, service level agreements, and performance monitoring systems that extend beyond the scope of the alliance contract (Hoetker & Mellewigt, 2009; Poppo & Zenger, 2002). Within this line of research, scholars interpreted relational norms as a complementary tool to legal contracts, jointly contributing to IORs' governance.

In a separate line of research influenced by sociology and organization theory, previous literature has underscored the importance of utilizing both formal and informal mechanisms in governing IORs. Within this field, formal structures encompass explicit organizational arrangements, while informal patterns involve implicit and uncodified rules of interaction and social dynamics for coordination. However, despite the extensive examination of the value and combined effects of formal and informal governance on firms' performance, the literature has often neglected to consider the significant influence of disruption on these mechanisms (Keller et al., 2021).

This chapter aims to examine various forms of governance and their implications for IORs, taking into account the impact of disruption. Additionally, we will explore the value of these different governance mechanisms. To provide concrete examples and insights, we will focus on the dynamic and rapidly evolving automotive industry, which is currently experiencing a disruptive technological change characterized by the transition to electric vehicles (EVs). The automotive context is particularly interesting as it allows us to consider not only the substitution of existing relationships but also the transformation of relationships with partners within a single industry. By studying the automotive industry, we can gain a deeper understanding of the dynamics and interactions between governance mechanisms and IORs in the face of disruption.

1.2 Exploring the Landscape: Unravelling the Typology of Governance Mechanisms in Interorganizational Relationships

The typology of governance mechanisms for IORs provide a comprehensive framework for understanding the diverse approaches taken to govern these complex collaborative arrangements. In this section, we delve into the intricacies of this typology, aiming to unravel the multifaceted nature of governance mechanisms employed in IORs. By exploring the classification proposed in the existing literature (Keller et al., 2021), we shed light on the different dimensions and perspectives that underpin the governance of interorganizational relationships. This exploration will enable us to gain a deeper understanding of how these mechanisms function, interact, and evolve within the dynamic landscape of IORs.

Before delving into an exploration of governance typology, it is necessary to establish some definitions. The literature on governance mechanisms for IORs often employs different conceptual labels, leading to variations in terminology. In previous research, the terms "contractual" and "formal" governance have largely been used interchangeably. For instance, Poppo and Zenger (2002) define "formal contracts" as legally binding written agreements. Similarly, Hoetker and Mellewigt (2009) encompass a broader scope with their definition of "formal mechanisms," which includes all written and documented interfaces utilized by partners in IORs to coordinate, cooperate, and monitor joint activities, extending beyond the confines of the alliance contract. On the other hand, informal governance are defined as agreements with no means of self-enforcing, relying on trust and reputation between the parties (Dyer & Singh, 1998). Poppo and Zenger (2002) go further in defining them as "the enforcement of obligations, promises, and expectations [that] occurs through social processes that promote norms of flexibility, solidarity, and information exchange" (Adler, 2001, p. 710).

To understand the dynamics and evolution of governance mechanisms, we offer a perspective that encompasses diverse dimensions concerning these mechanisms. Building on the work of Keller et al. (2021), we introduce a typology that distinguishes between the mechanisms used to enforce governance in IORs and the level of codification of these mechanisms.

The first dimension of governance in IORs centres on how partners intentionally structure their relationships to effectively enforce governance. Within this dimension, scholars have identified two key means of governance enforcement: the contractual and relational mechanisms. Contractual governance, as examined by Reuer and Ariño (2002) and reviewed by Schepker et al. (2014), focuses on the role of formal and written contracts that establish binding agreements between collaborating firms. These contracts explicitly outline responsibilities, obligations, and rights, serving as safeguards against self-interested behaviour, value appropriation, and future uncertainties. The extent of contract completeness has also been studied, linking it to the coverage of contingencies and the level of protection it provides. However, it is acknowledged that complete contracts may struggle to account for unforeseen contingencies, leading to the negotiation and development of rules governing IORs. These rules encompass not only complete contracts but also policies supplemented by other instrumental monitoring rules.

Conversely, relational mechanisms centre on the impact of social norms that govern behaviour within IORs. Scholars such as Lusch and Brown (1996) and Dyer and Singh (1998) have investigated how these norms shape expected behaviours and foster mutually beneficial relationships. Relational mechanisms rely on self-enforcement and emphasize the significance of trust and reliability in mitigating collaboration risks, facilitating coordination efforts, and promoting the exchange of information and knowledge among alliance partners.

In addition to the differentiation of enforcement mechanisms, Keller et al. (2021) introduce a second dimension in their typology of governance mechanisms, which focuses on the varying levels of codification of ruling principles within interorganizational relationships (McEvily et al., 2014). Some agreements may be formal and extensively documented, while others may be informal or based on verbal agreements and handshakes (P. Ring, 2002; P. S. Ring & Van de Ven, 1994). The level of codification reflects the degree to which the governance mechanisms are explicitly defined and recorded.

Formal mechanisms, for their specific nature, require documentation and updating as circumstances change, involving elaborate procedures and approvals. This enables accurate information on the timing and extent of changes, which can be collected, analysed, and used as data. On the other hand, informal mechanisms are sustained and transmitted through socialization with partners, establishing standards of appropriateness that discourage individual opportunism. If widely known and accepted, these informal mechanisms are often virtually self-enforcing and contribute to the reproduction of a social structure.

This typology of governance mechanisms provides invaluable insights into understanding their dynamics. The rules encompassing these mechanisms encompass explicit or implicit norms, regulations, and expectations that govern partner behaviour and interactions. Partners' actions are guided not only by anticipating uncertain consequences but also by a logic of appropriateness shaped by the structure of these rules. Rather than being strictly competitive or mutually exclusive, these perspectives on governance mechanisms are generally regarded as intertwined, recognizing their interconnected nature.

Having provided an overview of the typology and dynamics of governance mechanisms in IORs, we address discrepancies in conceptual labels and highlight different perspectives on governance mechanisms by exploring the classification proposed in the existing literature. The typology presented distinguishes between contractual and relational mechanisms as enforcement means for governance and explores their interplay. Additionally, it highlights the differentiation in the levels of codification of these mechanisms, whether formal or informal. This typology enables us to take a step forward in understanding the dynamics of governance mechanisms, thereby enhancing our comprehension of how they evolve and adapt within IORs. By delving into the intricacies of these mechanisms, researchers and practitioners can gain insights into their contingent value and effectiveness, enabling informed decision-making and strategic choices to sustain collaboration and achieve desired outcomes.

In the following sections of this chapter, we will delve deeper into the sources of turbulence that can impact the value of governance mechanisms, reviewing relevant literature and discussing their implications for managing change and ensuring effective collaboration within IORs. By advancing our knowledge in this field, we aim to contribute to the existing literature and provide practical insights for organizations engaged in interorganizational relationships.

1.3 Disruption in Inter-organizational Relationships

The theory of disruptive innovation, initially proposed by Christensen (1997), has emerged as one of the most influential frameworks for comprehending how firms and industries navigate technological change. Its significance is evident not only in academic circles but also in the practical realm, where practitioners have keenly examined the strategies employed by notable disruptors such as Google, Amazon, Uber, and Airbnb. However, while significant attention has been devoted to understanding the strategies of incumbents and the dynamics of disruption within industries, there remains a critical oversight in comprehending the impact of disruptive innovation on IORs. Specifically, the interplay between disruptive forces and the governance of IORs warrants closer examination, as it unveils the need for strategies that can effectively adapt and adjust interorganizational relationships in the face of these transformative changes. This section aims to bridge this gap by exploring the implications of disruptive innovation on IORs and delving into the strategies necessary to navigate and thrive amidst such disruptions.

The term "disruptions" encompasses a spectrum of shocks or changes that occur within the environment in which transacting parties operate. These disruptions have the potential to redefine the competitive landscape and render a firm's specific competencies less relevant, if not entirely obsolete. They can arise from a variety of factors, including breakthrough technologies, supply-side shocks, shifts in customer demand and preferences, and new industry regulations or deregulations (Kim & Prescott, 2005; Tripsas, 1997). Furthermore, disruptions can take on a more "mundane" form, resulting from errors of inattention, misalignment of actions, or failure to apply full effort (Simon, 1973). Whether stemming from major shocks or seemingly minor disturbances, disruptions can profoundly impact the scope of partnerships or the timely completion of partnership projects, potentially jeopardizing the very survival of the partnership itself (Mishra & Sinha, 2016). Understanding the ramifications of such disruptions on interorganizational relationships is crucial for devising effective strategies to navigate and mitigate their adverse effects.

The existing studies investigating the impact of disruptive changes on interorganizational relationships have predominantly focused on two main areas: examining the forms of governance that can anticipate and address these hazards and exploring the processes through which partners enhance coordination and cooperation to influence long-term performance.

The first approach, rooted in transaction cost economics, centres on the transaction itself and the role that governance mechanisms play in ensuring the success of the partnership (Williamson, 1991). This perspective highlights the significance of the initial structural design of a transaction in explaining alliance performance (Hennart, 2006). However, as circumstances evolve, the constraints imposed by the governance choices made during the formation of the transaction may limit a firm's ability to adapt to changing conditions (Argyres & Liebeskind, 1999). It is crucial to note that inefficiency is not necessarily inherent in this account. Rather, a focus on the individual transaction may reveal that firms exhibit a form of path dependency whereby history matters not because it generates inefficiencies per se, but because reversing certain commitments becomes prohibitively costly (Liebowitz & Margolis, 1995).

Despite the insights offered by the transaction cost economics perspective, it is essential to consider the limitations associated with an exclusive focus on governance mechanisms. A comprehensive understanding of the impact of disruptive innovation on interorganizational relationships necessitates an examination of the processes and dynamics within these relationships. Such an analysis delves into the coordination and cooperation strategies developed by partnering firms to improve performance over time.

By focusing solely on governance mechanisms, the transaction cost economics perspective may overlook the dynamic nature of interorganizational relationships and the need for adaptive strategies. In contrast, exploring the processes within relationships provides insights into how partners evolve their interactions and adjust their collaborative efforts in response to disruptive changes. By fostering effective coordination and cooperation, partnering firms can enhance their ability to navigate the challenges posed by disruptive innovation and ensure the longevity of their interorganizational relationships.

Another perspective that has gained attention in the study of interorganizational relationships focuses on the processes and dynamics that characterize these relationships. Within this perspective, researchers have directed their attention toward understanding the relational content of transactions and their embeddedness. Embeddedness refers to the extent to which social and economic relationships are intertwined and interconnected. Firms are considered embedded when they demonstrate a preference for engaging in economic transactions with other firms (Granovetter, 1985). These types of exchanges have been argued to foster private knowledge transfer due to the presence of trust and reciprocity, creating an environment where both parties can benefit from the transfer of knowledge (Uzzi, 1999).

By examining the relational content of interorganizational transactions and the level of embeddedness between partnering firms, scholars have sought to uncover the mechanisms through which trust and reciprocity facilitate knowledge sharing and collaboration. The presence of trust and reciprocity encourages firms to engage in cooperative behaviours, as they believe that their partners will act in a mutually beneficial manner. This promotes knowledge transfer that is conducted in a manner that respects the interests and needs of both parties involved. As a result, interorganizational relationships characterized by trust and reciprocity are more likely to effectively leverage and share valuable knowledge, fostering innovation and enhancing the overall performance of the partnership.

Understanding the dynamics of interorganizational relationships and the role of trust and reciprocity in facilitating knowledge transfer is vital in the context of disruptive innovation. As disruptions occur and challenge the existing order, partnerships that exhibit high levels of embeddedness and foster trust and reciprocity are better equipped to adapt to the changing circumstances. The strong foundation of trust and mutual benefit allows partners to manoeuvre through the uncertainties and complexities associated with disruptive forces, leading to more effective collaboration and ultimately enhancing the resilience and longevity of the interorganizational relationship.

While the previous perspectives have shed light on the impact of disruptive forces on IORs, particularly in terms of reduced interpersonal trust and increased uncertainty (Bendapudi & Leone, 2002; Palmatier, 2008), it is important to recognize that the solutions proposed within these perspectives are not independent of one another. Instead, they are inherently linked and mutually influential, operating within and between transactions. Researchers have demonstrated the interconnected nature of structural and relational aspects, revealing how they mutually shape each other's dynamics within and across transactions (Faems et al., 2008). This finding emphasizes the interdependence of governance mechanisms and relational dynamics, highlighting the need to consider both perspectives simultaneously.

In examining the interplay between governance mechanisms and relational dynamics, studies have uncovered a range of roles that these factors can assume within interorganizational relationships. They can act as substitutes or complements, exerting influence at different levels, including partnering organizations as a whole and specific groups of individuals within these organizations (Brattström & Faems, 2020; Schilke & Cook, 2013). Such research highlights the complexity of managing interorganizational relationships in the face of disruptive innovation, as different factors and actors interact to shape the overall effectiveness and outcomes of these relationships.

By recognizing the interconnections between governance mechanisms, relational dynamics, and their multi-faceted roles, a more comprehensive understanding of how to address the challenges posed by disruptive forces in IORs can be attained. This integrative approach enables researchers and practitioners to develop strategies that leverage the interplay between governance mechanisms and relational dynamics, fostering resilience, adaptability, and innovative outcomes in the face of disruptive innovation.

In conclusion, this section has addressed critical gaps in existing research by examining the impact of disruptive innovation on interorganizational relationships. By delving into the interplay between disruptive forces and the governance mechanisms and relational dynamics within IORs, we have shed light on the need for strategies that can effectively adapt and adjust these relationships in the face of transformative changes. Our study brings together two essential elements that have been overlooked in previous research: (1) a detailed analysis of contingent factors that influence the structuring of efficient governance mechanisms, particularly those related to collaborating firms, and their influence on uncertainty levels and transaction-specific investments, as well as the relative effectiveness of contractual and relational governance; (2) an exploration of the dynamics that characterize the evolution of governance within and across interorganizational relationships.

By integrating these perspectives, our study contributes to a more comprehensive understanding of the challenges and opportunities presented by disruptive innovation in IORs. The fine-grained analysis of contingencies factors helps identify the contextual factors that shape the selection and effectiveness of governance mechanisms, allowing for tailored approaches that consider the specific characteristics of the collaboration and its associated uncertainty. Furthermore, studying the dynamics of governance within and across relationships reveals how these governance structures evolve over time and adapt to disruptive forces, providing insights into the mechanisms through which interorganizational relationships can remain resilient and foster innovation.

Overall, our research highlights the importance of addressing the interconnections between disruptive forces, governance mechanisms, and relational dynamics in order to navigate the complexities of interorganizational relationships amidst disruptive innovation. By taking into account the contingencies factors and understanding the dynamic nature of governance within and across relationships, organizations can develop strategies that enhance their ability to adapt, thrive, and foster innovation in the face of disruptive change.

1.4 Exploring the Transformation of the Automotive Industry: A Methodological Clarification

We aim to complete the analysis of the challenges of governing IORs for innovation in times of disruption using a case study of the automotive industry. The changing automotive ecosystem is particularly attractive for two reasons. First, it allows us to illustrate the impact of strong transformation within the context of a single industry that, despite many substantial technological modifications in the knowledge base, still does not seem subject to major disruptions. Incumbents still hold strong positions and no significant new entrant has challenged their dominant innovative position (Bergek et al., 2013). Second, the changing automotive ecosystem provides a fertile context to study IORs governance mechanisms, since its innovation processes along the supply-chain have been traditionally based on collaborative IORs. As the industry experiences transformation, examining IORs governance in this dynamic context allows us to understand how governance adapts and evolves in response to industry changes. Our proposed methodological approach that departs from previous research will provide more fine-grained analysis of how IORs are governed during industry evolution. This will contribute new insights into IORs governance sophistication and help address open questions about IORs governance amidst industry disruption.

With regards to the first point, the automotive industry was viewed as technologically mature, following a post dominant design path that was increasingly evolutionary and incremental (Abernathy & Utterback, 1978). By contrast, today's automotive industry has been going a series of radical change that might impact the structure of its entire ecosystem. Indeed, the electrification of the vehicle powertrain, the autonomous driving, the shared-use mobility platforms, and data connectivity might impact the role of incumbent that should have been displaced if we accept the analogy with the fate of the PC in recent decades (Jacobides & MacDuffie, 2013). While many of the incumbent global automakers such as Toyota, GM, Ford, Volkswagen, and BMW—commonly called original equipment manufacturers (OEMs)—have so far maintained their central positions, a key question is how the structure of current ecosystem of IORs will be disrupted by new entrants such as Tesla, Waymo and others, which are attempting to leverage new technologies.

Previous studies have described the IORs relationships in the automotive sectors in details. For instance, Mudambi and Helper (1998) posited a model of close but adversarial buyer–supplier relations in the U.S. auto industry, while Helper and Henderson (2014) remark how the automakers' relationships in the US were also very different from those of their Japanese competitors. They were characterized by short-term - usually one-year—contracts, arms'-length relationships, and a reliance on as many as six to eight suppliers per part (MacDuffie & Helper, 1997). While this belief did not promote quality, it did facilitate the maintenance of "spot" relationships with suppliers. The differences that scholars have observes in the different contexts reinforce the idea that few aspects of the governance contextual features survive when these practices are transferred. Therefore, it is important to analyse the heterogeneity of the forms of IORs governance not only across the different firms but also across the relationships a firm establishes.

In order to provide detailed and accurate account of the form of governance across the firms' interorganisational relationships we developed methodological approach that differ from the traditional analysis of governance mechanism on the subsequent points. First, we collected a detailed account of the characteristics of the firms' IOR, and of their governance modes and changes. Second, while previous studies have traditionally focused on the characteristics of dyads (length, strength, governance arrangement, etc.) or the features of the alliance portfolio (variety/similarity, numerosity of relations, etc.), we conducted a cross-sectional analysis of the three most important relationships for each firm and we independently evaluated the IOR portfolio and the IOR network characteristics for each firm (Wang & Rajagopalan, 2015). Third, as IORs involve processes through which partnerships are formed, managed, changed, and terminated, we examined the evolution of these forms. Time is therefore another structuring element of our analysis of IORs' governance (Mitchell & James, 2001; Shi et al., 2012). This approach allowed us to have a pluralistic approach to the analysis of these IORs that could take into account the power of the governance mechanisms that we can attribute at each level as well as the nature of the dynamics nested across the different levels of analysis.

1.5 Overview of the Book

The chapters in this book explore how to manage inter-organizational relationship and what are the strategies that support their development during times of disruption. In Chapter 2, the theoretical analysis provides an account of how to design the form of governance given the hazard of the relationship. The different characteristics at the dyad, portfolio, and network level explain how the behavioural uncertainty that arises from the unpredictability of actions in disrupted relationships, shedding light on decision-making processes and the role of uncertainty in IORs.

In the Chapter 3, we emphasize the significance of adaptation in response to disruptions, highlighting the actions taken to ensure project's or transaction's progress despite the challenges faced. The authors extensively examine the complexities involved in managing and adapting to disruptions in alliances. They achieve this through a comprehensive analysis of disruptive events and their effects on knowledge loss, interpersonal trust, and uncertainty. Moreover, they explore specific disruptions arising from technological advancements and regulatory changes. Recognizing that not all disruptions are drastic shocks but rather a collection of mundane disruptions, the book examines the cumulative effects of these seemingly minor disturbances and their impact on project delivery and overall success. By uncovering the underlying causes of disruptions and their implications, this volume offers valuable insights into managing and mitigating the risks associated with disruptions in IORs.

Ultimately, the overarching goal of this book is to enhance our understanding of how technological disruption influences alliance governance mechanisms. By synthesizing existing research and presenting novel perspectives, it aims to equip scholars, practitioners, and policymakers with the knowledge and tools needed to navigate the complexities of disruptions and foster resilient and adaptive interorganizational relationships.

In the Chapter 4, the case study of the automotive industry show that as technological advancements continue to reshape industries and disrupt traditional business models, it is imperative to comprehend the transformative power of disruptions. This book serves as a valuable resource for researchers and professionals alike, enabling them to navigate the turbulent waters of technological disruption and forge robust IORs in an ever-evolving business landscape.

Chapter 5 concludes the book highlighting its main empirical and theoretical contributions. In conclusion, this book provides a timely and comprehensive exploration of the design and development of governance mechanisms for interorganizational relationships. Through its diverse range of contributions, it offers insights, frameworks, and strategies for effectively managing disruptions and foster resilient alliances in the face of technological change.

References

Abernathy, W. J., & Utterback, J. M. (1978). Patterns of industrial innovation. *Technology Review, 80*(7), 40–47.

Adler, P. S. (2001). Market, hierarchy, and trust: The knowledge economy and the future of capitalism. *Organization Science, 12*(2), 215–234.

Ansari, S. S., Garud, R., & Kumaraswamy, A. (2016). The disruptor's dilemma: TiVo and the U.S. television ecosystem: The Disruptor's Dilemma. *Strategic Management Journal, 37*(9), 1829–1853. https://doi.org/10.1002/smj.2442

Argyres, N. S., & Liebeskind, J. P. (1999). Contractual commitments, bargaining power, and governance inseparability: Incorporating history into transaction cost theory. *Academy of Management Review, 24*(1), 49–63.

Bendapudi, N., & Leone, R. P. (2002). Managing business-to-business customer relationships following key contact employee turnover in a vendor firm. *Journal of Marketing, 66*(2), 83–101. https://doi.org/10.1509/jmkg.66.2.83.18476

Bergek, A., Berggren, C., Magnusson, T., & Hobday, M. (2013). Technological discontinuities and the challenge for incumbent firms: Destruction, disruption or creative accumulation? *Research Policy, 42*(6), 1210–1224. https://doi.org/10.1016/j.respol.2013.02.009

Brandenburger, A. M., & Nalebuff, B. J. (1997). *Co-opetition*. New York: Doubleday.

Brattström, A., & Faems, D. (2020). Interorganizational relationships as political battlefields: How fragmentation within organizations shapes relational dynamics between organizations. *Academy of Management Journal, 63*(5), 1591–1620. https://doi.org/10.5465/amj.2018.0038

Cao, L., Mohan, K., Ramesh, B., & Sarkar, S. (2013). Evolution of governance: Achieving ambidexterity in IT outsourcing. *Journal of Management Information Systems, 30*(3), 115–140.

Christensen, C. M. (1997). *The innovator's dilemma: When new technologies cause great firms to fail*. Harvard Business School Press.

Dyer, J. H., & Singh, H. (1998). The relational view: Cooperative strategy and sources of interorganizational competitive advantage. *The Academy of Management Review, 23*(4), 660–679. http://www.jstor.org/stable/259056

Faems, D., Janssens, M., Madhok, A., & Looy, B. (2008). Toward an integrative perspective on alliance governance: Connecting contract design, trust dynamics, and contract application. *The Academy of Management Journal.* https://doi.org/10.5465/AMJ.2008.35732527

Furr, N., & Shipilov, A. (2018). Building the right ecosystem for innovation. *MIT Sloan Management Review, 59*(4), 59–64. https://www.proquest.com/docview/2057218988/abstract/AAB23D0896254344PQ/1

Granovetter, M. (1985). Economic action and social structure: The problem of embeddedness. *American Journal of Sociology, 91*(3), 481–510.

Helper, S., & Henderson, R. (2014). Management practices, relational contracts, and the decline of general motors. *Journal of Economic Perspectives, 28*(1), 49–72. https://doi.org/10.1257/jep.28.1.49

Hennart, J.-F. (2006). Alliance research: Less is more*. *Journal of Management Studies, 43*(7), 1621–1628. https://doi.org/10.1111/j.1467-6486.2006.00654.x

Hoetker, G., & Mellewigt, T. (2009). Choice and performance of governance mechanisms: Matching alliance governance to asset type. *Strategic Management Journal, 30*(10), 1025–1044. https://doi.org/10.1002/smj.775

Jacobides, M. G., & MacDuffie, J. P. (2013). How to drive value your way. *Harvard Business Review, 91*(7), 92–100.

Kapoor, R., & Lee, J. M. (2013). Coordinating and competing in ecosystems: How organizational forms shape new technology investments. *Strategic Management Journal, 34*(3), 274–296. https://doi.org/10.1002/smj.2010

Keller, A., Lumineau, F., Mellewigt, T., & Ariño, A. (2021). Alliance governance mechanisms in the face of disruption. *Organization Science, 32*(6), 1542–1570. https://doi.org/10.1287/orsc.2021.1437

Kim, B., & Prescott, J. E. (2005). Deregulatory forms, variations in the speed of governance adaptation, and firm performance. *The Academy of Management Review, 30*(2), 414–425. https://www.jstor.org/stable/20159127

Liebowitz, S. J., & Margolis, S. E. (1995). Path dependence, lock-in, and history. *The Journal of Law, Economics, and Organization, 11*(1), 205–226.

Lusch, R. F., & Brown, J. R. (1996). Interdependency, contracting, and relational behavior in marketing channels. *Journal of Marketing, 60*(4), 19–38. https://doi.org/10.1177/002224299606000404

MacDuffie, J. P., & Helper, S. (1997). Creating lean suppliers: Diffusing lean production through the supply chain. *California Management Review, 39*(4), 118–151. https://doi.org/10.2307/41165913

McEvily, B., Soda, G., & Tortoriello, M. (2014). More formally: Rediscovering the missing link between formal organization and informal social structure. *Academy of Management Annals, 8*(1), 299–345.

Mishra, A., & Sinha, K. K. (2016). Work design and integration glitches in globally distributed technology projects. *Production and Operations Management, 25*(2), 347–369. https://doi.org/10.1111/poms.12425

Mitchell, T. R., & James, L. R. (2001). Building better theory: Time and the specification of when things happen. *The Academy of Management Review, 26*(4), 530–547. https://doi.org/10.2307/3560240

Mudambi, R., & Helper, S. (1998). The 'close but adversarial' model of supplier relations in the U.S. auto industry. *Strategic Management Journal, 19*(8), 775–792. https://doi.org/10.1002/(SICI)1097-0266(199808)19:8<775::AID-SMJ970>3.0.CO;2-V

Palmatier, R. W. (2008). Interfirm relational drivers of customer value. *Journal of Marketing, 72*(4), 76–89. https://doi.org/10.1509/jmkg.72.4.076

Poppo, L., & Zenger, T. (2002). Do formal contracts and relational governance function as substitutes or complements? *Strategic Management Journal, 23*(8), 707–725. https://doi.org/10.1002/smj.249

Reuer, J. J., & Ariño, A. (2002). Contractual renegotiations in strategic alliances. *Journal of Management, 28*(1), 47–68.

Ring, P. (2002). The role of contract in strategic alliances. *Cooperative Strategies and Alliances*, 145–162.

Ring, P. S., & Van de Ven, A. H. (1994). Developmental processes of cooperative interorganizational relationships. *Academy of Management Review, 19*(1), 90–118.

Schepker, D. J., Oh, W.-Y., Martynov, A., & Poppo, L. (2014). The many futures of contracts: Moving beyond structure and safeguarding to coordination and adaptation. *Journal of Management, 40*(1), 193–225. https://doi.org/10.1177/0149206313491289

Schilke, O., & Cook, K. S. (2013). A cross-level process theory of trust development in interorganizational relationships. *Strategic Organization, 11*(3), 281–303. https://doi.org/10.1177/1476127012472096

Shi, W., Sun, J., & Prescott, J. E. (2012). A temporal perspective of merger and acquisition and strategic alliance initiatives: Review and future direction. *Journal of Management, 38*(1), 164–209. https://doi.org/10.1177/0149206311424942

Simon, H. A. (1973). The structure of ill structured problems. *Artificial Intelligence, 4*(3), 181–201. https://doi.org/10.1016/0004-3702(73)90011-8

Tripsas, M. (1997). Unraveling the process of creative destruction: Complementary assets and incumbent survival in the typesetter industry. *Strategic Management Journal, 18*(S1), 119–142. https://doi.org/10.1002/(SICI)1097-0266(199707)18:1+%3c119::AID-SMJ921%3e3.0.CO;2-0

Uzzi, B. (1999). Embeddedness in the making of financial capital: How social relations and networks benefit firms seeking financing. *American Sociological Review, 64*(4), 481–505.

Wang, Y., & Rajagopalan, N. (2015). Alliance capabilities: Review and research agenda. *Journal of Management, 41*(1), 236–260. https://doi.org/10.1177/0149206314557157

Williamson, O. E. (1979). Transaction-cost economics: The governance of contractual relations. *Journal of Law and Economics, 22*(2), 29. http://www.jstor.org/stable/725118

Williamson, O. E. (1991). Comparative economic organization: The analysis of discrete structural alternatives. *Administrative Science Quarterly, 36*(2), 269–296. http://www.jstor.org/stable/2393356

Zollo, M., Reuer, J. J., & Singh, H. (2002). Interorganizational routines and performance in strategic alliances. *Organization Science, 13*(6), 701–713. https://doi.org/10.1287/orsc.13.6.701.503

CHAPTER 2

Exchange Hazards and Governance Choices

Abstract This chapter explores the challenges of collaborative innovation strategies for firms, focusing on partners' features and governance choices. The distributed innovation context increases the complexity of cooperation and coordination, posing governance challenges. The analysis considers three levels: the dyad, IORs portfolio, and network, highlighting how governance mechanisms vary in value depending on partner nature, portfolio characteristics, and network structure. Previous research has examined how relational and contractual governance mechanisms interact, affecting performance and exchange hazards in IORs. Exchange hazards, associated with uncertainty and transaction-specific investments, are particularly relevant in collaborative innovation contexts. The conclusion reveals that the value of governance mechanisms differs across levels of analysis, emphasizing the need for firms to develop relational capabilities to explore the complexities of collaborative innovation effectively.

Keywords Collaborative innovation · Exchange hazards · Governance challenges · Relational governance · Contractual governance

---

© The Author(s), under exclusive license to Springer Nature Switzerland AG 2024
S. Li Pira and A. Moretti, *Governing Interorganizational Relationships for Innovation*,
https://doi.org/10.1007/978-3-031-50229-3_2

2.1 CONTRACTUAL AND RELATIONAL GOVERNANCE AND EXCHANGE HAZARDS

This chapter addresses two crucial concerns in firms' collaborative innovation strategies: with *whom* to cooperate and *how* to govern the relationship. As introduced by Chapter 1, the distributed innovation context amplifies the complexity of cooperation and coordination, leading to significant governance challenges. To unravel this complexity, it becomes necessary to distinguish between three levels of analysis: the dyad, the portfolio of interorganizational relationships (IORs), and the network level. These levels provide insights into how the value of governance mechanisms can change based on the nature of dyadic partners, characteristics of the focal firm's IORs portfolio, and the overall network structure.

Previous literature has extensively examined effective governance of IORs for innovation, particularly focusing on dyadic characteristics. Scholars have discussed how relational and contractual governance mechanisms can vary in effectiveness, their mutual relationship, and their joint impact on dyadic performance (Cao & Lumineau, 2015) and the *exchange hazards* associated with IORs (Abdi & Aulakh, 2017; Oliver, 1990; Rindfleisch, 2000).

Exchange hazards, typically linked to uncertainty (Abdi & Aulakh, 2017) and transaction-specific investments (Noordewier et al., 1990; Uzzi, 1997), are recognized as major causes of "economic exchange problems" (Williamson, 1975) and the main drivers behind governance theories (Gulati & Zajac, 1998). These dimensions hold particular relevance in collaborative innovation contexts where (i) uncertainty surrounding innovative projects prevents pre-defining the objects/tasks to be exchanged, (ii) joint projects often necessitate partners sharing proprietary knowledge to some extent, and (iii) costly investments, subject to a certain level of risk, are typically involved.

Generally, when exchange hazards are intense, relying on relational governance mechanisms may become challenging for partners (Abdi & Aulakh, 2017; Rindfleisch, 2000), and contractual arrangements may decline in their effectiveness for coordination and control functions (Malhotra & Lumineau, 2011; Reuer & Ariño, 2002). Other scholars have noted that when exchange hazards cannot be mitigated through formal contracts, relational governance becomes the means to enhance mutual safeguards against opportunistic behaviors. However, relying on relational governance entails significant costs, as it restricts access to new information and opportunities (Gargiulo & Benassi, 2000; Uzzi, 1997). Thus, relational governance proves effective and valuable primarily when exchange hazards are intense (Poppo & Zenger, 2002).

2.2 Governing Collaborations at the Dyad Level

Previous literature has underscored the significance of both partners' characteristics (Azadegan, 2011; Esper et al., 2010; Hult et al., 2007; von Hippel, 1988) and relationship attributes (Adler et al., 2009; Sanders, 2008; Villena et al., 2011) in influencing exchange hazards. The subsequent sections examine how these features are connected to the effectiveness of various governance mechanisms (Eckerd et al., 2021).

2.2.1 Partners' Features and Exchange Hazards

Understanding which partners' features affect exchange hazards can help exploring the question: *How does the value of governance mechanisms change depending on the partners' characteristics?* Based on previous literature, we identify four main dimensions over which we can differentiate the value of governance mechanisms in relation to the type of IORs' partners (Albers et al., 2016): partners' relative position along the supply chain (Baum et al., 2000; Rindfleisch, 2000; Villena & Craighead, 2017), size (Villena & Craighead, 2017), power and dependence (Gulati & Sytch, 2007; Lee & Johnsen, 2012; Terpend & Ashenbaum, 2012), and cultural distance (Burkert et al., 2012; Li et al., 2010).

Position along the supply-chain. Scholars exploring the issue of governance mechanisms' effectiveness considering partners' relative position along the supply-chain mainly focused on buyer–supplier relationships, exploring the ways in which governance configuration impacts on the IOR's performance (Terpend & Ashenbaum, 2012). In particular, previous research focused on the idea that buying firms would preferably rely on contractual governance through which they can set up both control and coordination mechanisms with their suppliers (Lumineau & Henderson, 2012): through contracts, they can reduce uncertainty and objectivity in exchanges and coordination can be preserved thanks to contractual clarifications and norms useful to counter against dysfunctional events (Villena et al., 2021). From buyers' point of view, contracts not only serve as a safeguard against suppliers' noncompliance, but they can also include clauses useful for the supply manager monitoring and controlling activities (Villena et al., 2021). The reduction of uncertainty brought by the formal agreements has been showed also conducive of buyers' higher willingness to develop exploratory innovation with suppliers, thanks to the possibility to anticipate a future together (Gupta et al., 2006). While the literature did not explicit tackled the changing effectiveness of governance mechanisms depending on the directionality of the relationship (being a supplier or a client), the well-known hold-up problem defines a clear theoretical framework from the suppliers' perspective, especially if involved in a commitment-intensive alliance with an R&D component (Oxley, 1997). When contracts are incomplete, as they usually are in the innovation domain for the above-mentioned complexities, suppliers are subject to potential opportunistic behaviors of their clients, and incentives for cooperation are attenuated (Williamson, 1985, 1991). Complementing the contractual governance with relational mechanisms can thus be necessary to overcome problems related to transaction-specific investments (Poppo & Zenger, 2002).

Size. Partners' relative size has been discussed as a potential source of exchange hazards, especially when the two partners are asymmetric (Johnsen & Ford, 2008). In particular, size asymmetry has been described by Villena and Craighead (2017) as a source of uncertainty for three main reasons: interpretative uncertainty, unbalanced resources, bargaining power. The underlying assumption for all these reasons is that firms' size is a proxy for each partners' management styles (Claycomb & Frankwick, 2004), cognitive frames (Weber & Mayer, 2014), and available resources for bargaining and negotiations (Williamson, 1996): when the two parties have different sizes, they differ under all these dimensions, thus collaboration is characterized by high levels of exchange hazards related mainly to uncertainty (Lee & Johnsen, 2012). Larger firms are usually adopting more formal and bureaucratic forms of communication and interactions then smaller counterpart that, conversely, can interpret this formal approach as opportunistic (Villena & Craighead, 2017). Smaller firms, if required to invest in transaction-specific assets, will suffer from high uncertainty regarding the good intentions of the larger companies, that could be tempted to capitalize on their larger resources to get more information about the exchange (Moriarty Jr & Spekman, 1984): in this case, contractual arrangements, if not complete, would be necessarily complemented by the use of relational governance, in order to lower opportunism perception by the smaller partner of the transaction

(Lumineau et al., 2022). Moreover, larger endowments of resources could result in higher bargaining power of the larger firm over the smaller one (Crook & Combs, 2007): even in this case, the small firm would not be reassured by contractual arrangements on the goodwill of their partner, and more social and informal means of governance will be necessary (Hingley, 2005; Johnsen & Ford, 2008; Lee & Johnsen, 2012).

Cultural distance. When partners belong to different cultural backgrounds, inter-organizational relationships have been found to be more complex to govern because of the higher uncertainty arising with cultural distance (Burkert et al., 2012; Cao & Lumineau, 2015; Fryxell et al., 2002). As noted by Abdi and Aulakh (2017), cross-border collaborations are characterized by socio-cognitive differences that result in idiosyncratic expectations (Abdi & Aulakh, 2012), difficulties in assessing partners' efficiency (Luo, 2005), reliance on different social norms and meanings (Dyer & Nobeoka, 2000), and degraded common grounds (Srikanth & Puranam, 2011). In such a context, coordination and control functions are particularly difficult to develop having as a consequence an increased behavioral uncertainty (Zhao et al., 2004). When partners experience behavioral uncertainty, contractual arrangements help especially in the coordination function, defining norms for interaction and joint projects development. Simultaneously, contractual arrangements can serve as a means for both partners to mitigate the risks associated with potential opportunistic behavior, which may arise due to the inherent uncertainty inherent in the transaction. As a result, such arrangements enhance the effectiveness of the control function. In the context of relationships characterized by significant cultural divergence, the establishment of relational mechanisms would prove prohibitively expensive. Moreover, partners, guided by distinct social norms and interpretations, are likely to exhibit reduced effectiveness in this regard.

Power/Dependence. As proposed by Lee and Johnsen (2012), we conceive power and dependence as two faces of the same coin. Power, in fact, is the extent to which one partner can get the other one to do something that it would not otherwise have done (Dahl, 2005; Hausman & Johnston, 2010). On the other side, dependence is the opposite of power: the more one partner depends on the other, the less power it can exert on it (Emerson, 1981; Hingley, 2005). Power and dependence have been found to be problematic for IORs when they are asymmetric between the partners, thus requiring different governance arrangements to make up for exchange hazards linked to these asymmetries. In particular, the opportunity for the more powerful party to exploit the low-power one makes the latter uncertain about their counterparts' behavior, leading to potential dissatisfaction about the relationship (Anderson & Narus, 1984), less cooperation and greater conflict (Anderson & Weitz, 1989; Nyaga et al., 2013; Villena & Craighead, 2017). In relationships characterized by power asymmetries, relational governance can help the less powerful party overcoming conflict and low levels of communication, cooperation, trust and stability that would characterize the relationship if using the contractual arrangements only (Kumar et al., 1995). Moreover, the formal agreements could be perceived by the less powerful party as a means to enforce the counterpart's will, over which one can't exert any influence, thus negatively affecting the overall relationship's performance (Nyaga et al., 2013). A different situation occurs for jointly dependent partners, that are characterized by a non-adversarial nature (Dore, 1983). When IORs' partners are mutually dependent, relational mechanisms allow mutual adjustments and interorganizational learning that lead the partners to get superior economic returns (Gulati & Sytch, 2007; MacDuffie & Helper, 1997).

2.2.2 Relationship's Features and Exchange Hazards

As acknowledged by previous literature (Noordewier et al., 1990; Uzzi, 1997), exchange hazards are influenced also by relationships features. Exploring how these features affect uncertainty and transition-specific investments can help exploring the question: *How does the value of governance mechanisms change depending on the relationship's characteristics?* Leveraging past scholarly work, we organize relationships' features discussion into three main groups: relational embeddedness (Granovetter, 1985; Poppo & Zenger, 2002), multiplexity (Shipilov et al., 2014), trust (Eckerd et al., 2021; Graebner et al., 2020), and object of exchange (Cao & Lumineau, 2015).

Relational embeddedness. Rooted in Granovetter (1985)'s seminal work on embeddedness and social capital theory (Burt, 1997), the concept of relational embeddedness refers to the fact that economic behavior "is closely embedded in networks of inter personal relations" (Granovetter, 1985, p. 504), and emphasizes the role that "personal relations and structures (or 'networks') of such relations' play in the daily work and accomplishments of all sorts of economic actors" (Granovetter, 1985, p. 490). IORs can be thus characterized by their relational embeddedness, namely their length (Cao & Lumineau, 2015), strength (Poppo & Zenger, 2002), and multiple embeddedness (Shipilov et al., 2014). As the literature emphasized, depending on the IORs' embeddedness, the value of different governance mechanisms can change. Overall, scholars agree that relational embeddedness mitigates exchange hazards, increasing the effectiveness of relational governance. In particular, when relationships' length (in terms of number of years firms have been dealing with each other) is high, uncertainty about partners' behavior is reduced because they better know each other and with time they could have the opportunity to develop joint routines and shared norms of interaction; moreover, with increasing length of the relationships, partners may also enter into transaction-specific investments, reducing also the risk of being exploited by their counterparts (Mayer & Argyres, 2004; Wagner & Bode, 2014). Thus, given the positive effect of relational embeddedness on exchange hazards, relational governance's value increases, while contractual governance may result less effective. Scholars, in fact, emphasized that when partners are engaged with each other for a long time, the formal strings attached to contracts could be interpreted a signal of mistrust by the parties, and foster the atmosphere of distrust (Cao & Lumineau, 2015; Dyer, 1997; Fryxell et al., 2002). Similar governance values are those associated with relationships' strength, in terms of intensity of repeated exchanges (Sytch & Tatarynowicz, 2014) between the partners (that could, or could not, be directly related to relationship length). As noted by Poppo and Zenger (2002), both sociologists and economists noted that partners engaged in repeated exchanges are able to collect information (reduce uncertainty) about their counterparts' cooperative behavior and to make informed choices about trusting the partner with relationship-specific investments.

Multiplexity. Multiplexity is "the extent to which two actors are connected by more than one type of tie" (Kilduff & Tsai, 2003, p. 135): e.g., two organizations can be partners, competitors, members of the same business association at the same time. As noted by Shipilov et al. (2014), when IORs are characterized by multiplexity, the two partners can get greater flexibility in building network ties, more stable exchange relationships, and the ability to adopt tailored innovations. Moreover, multiplexity can also result in multiple valences (e.g., not only cooperative, but also conflictual) of the relationship, namely being conflictual and cooperative at the same time (Lumineau & Oliveira, 2018). When partners' relationship is stratified on several different types of ties, exchange hazards can be affected by a complex interaction between uncertainty and transaction-specific investments that characterize each tie. Understanding how multiplexity affects different governance mechanisms' value, however, has not been explored by the literature so far. It configures as a promising area for future research.

Trust. One of the most used definitions of trust in IORs literature is provided by Mayer et al. (1995, p. 712) and refers to "the willingness of one party to be vulnerable to the actions of another party", based upon positive expectations of its intentions or behavior (Rousseau et al., 1998). Trust has been acknowledged as one of the main factors mitigating exchange hazards: if the two partners of an IOR trust each other, uncertainty about each other's behaviors will be minimized, as well as the risk of being exploited by the counterpart if investing in transaction-specific investments (Cai et al., 2010; Zaheer & Venkatraman, 1995; Zaheer et al., 1998). This happens because trust becomes embedded in a particular IOR, and once the partner is labeled as trustworthy, it is expected to behave in accordance with shared social norms of cooperation and reciprocity (Graebner et al., 2020; Poppo & Zenger, 2002) Trust has been traditionally associated with relational governance (Poppo & Zenger, 2002), being one of its foundational characters (Cao & Lumineau, 2015; Nooteboom et al., 1997; Uzzi, 1997). However, as pragmatists noted, relational governance is possible also without trust (MacDuffie & Helper, 2007): joint practices and monitoring techniques make relational governance function also when the partners do not trust each other (Gulati & Sytch, 2007; Heide & John, 1990; Helper et al., 2000). Trust is then interpreted as a specific relationships' feature, and the literature emphasizes especially its positive relationship with relational governance: the higher the trust between the parties, the more effective and valuable will be relational governance (Keller et al., 2021). However, a more complex relation emerges between trust and contractual governance: as Eckerd et al. (2021) and Lumineau (2017) highlighted, only distinguishing between control and coordination functions of the contract we can have a consistent understanding of its relationship with trust. Trust will affect positively and will be, in turn, positively affected by the contracts' coordination functions while, conversely, it will reduce the value of (and it will be negatively affected by) contracts' control function (Lumineau, 2017).

Object of exchange. The relationship between two partners can vary also by the type of object to be exchanged by the parties. In particular, when the exchange between the parties is based on complex products, based on highly specialized knowledge, encompassing joint R&D, and where the parties cannot specify ex-ante the object's details, they will experience higher uncertainty and transaction-specific investments (Williamson, 1975, 1979). This is the usual context of IORs for innovation, where the object of exchange is, by definition, innovative, and the contracts are necessarily incomplete (Pisano, 1989). In this situation, contractual governance mechanisms have been found less effective (Cao & Lumineau, 2015; Gilson et al., 2009; Keller et al., 2021), and relational governance is usually addressed as a means for reducing partners' threat of being exploited by their counterparts' opportunistic behaviors (Howard et al., 2019; Keller et al., 2021; Malhotra & Lumineau, 2011).

2.3 Governing Collaborations at the Portfolio Level

The rich research developed on IORs has traditionally focused on the dyad as the unit of analysis; however, in the last decades, several scholars pointed out that the alliance portfolio as the unit of analysis can provide important insights on several issues related to firms' performance and competitiveness (Gulati, 1998; Lavie, 2006; Park & Zhou, 2005; Wassmer, 2010). As Wassmer (2010) observes, alliance portfolio has been defined by several theoretical lenses: from an additive approach where the alliance portfolio is the aggregate of all IORs of a focal firm (Bae & Gargiulo, 2004; George et al., 2001; Gulati et al., 2011), to the network literature defining an alliance portfolio as the focal firm's egocentric IORs network (Baum et al., 2000; Ozcan & Eisenhardt, 2009; Rowley et al., 2000). These definitions, and their slightly different connotations, highlight that it is possible to explore the implications of the characteristics of the alliance portfolio from two different perspectives: the portfolio and at the focal-firm levels. When several partners are collaborating with the same one, in fact, they are indirectly connected by their shared relationship with the focal firm. On the other hand, when a firm is engaged in a set of different IORs, its internal organizational processes and competences are shaped by the experience it is accumulating through the interaction with its partners via a process of reciprocal influence and interdependence: what is learnt with one partner can influence and address the firm's behavior with its other partners. Both these dynamics developing at the portfolio level can increase or mitigate IORs exchange hazards, influencing the (perceived) uncertainty and the transaction-specificity of the investments required to the focal firm and its partners. The next two subsections explore these two different perspectives, in order to contribute to answer to the question: *how does the value of governance mechanisms change depending on the firm's IORs portfolio?*

2.3.1 Exchange Hazards at the Portfolio Level

Only scant literature has noted that the alliance portfolio configuration, namely its content and arrangement, has important implications for the contingent value of governance mechanisms (Wassmer, 2010). However, when portfolios vary in size (Ahuja, 2000; Hoffmann, 2007), structural dimensions (breadth, density, redundancy) (Ahuja, 2000; Gulati & Gargiulo, 1999), tie strength (Hoffmann, 2007; Rowley et al., 2000), and partners' dimension and characteristics (Lavie, 2007; Stuart, 2000), their intrinsic interdependencies affect the effectiveness of different governance mechanisms. In particular, such interdependencies result in different levels of synergies and conflict between the focal firm's alliances (Vassolo et al., 2004; Wassmer, 2010), thus affecting the effectiveness of relational and contractual governance at the portfolio level.

Past contributions exploring synergies and conflict in alliance portfolios emphasized the framework of coopetition dynamics (Villena et al., 2021; Wilhelm & Sydow, 2018). In the work developed by Wilhelm and Sydow (2018), whose empirical research is grounded in the automotive industry, they find that a focal firm's capabilities to manage the coopetition dynamics characterizing its partners' portfolio are crucial to moderate conflicts and to create joint value from partners' collaboration. In their description of the carmakers' governance approach with their suppliers, they enumerate a number of contractual vs. relational arrangements adopted by these focal firms, showing how the ability to shift from the one to the other was critical for their IORs portfolio success.

In particular, when the competitive dynamics among the focal firm's partners are particularly intense (the Volkswagen case, in Wilhelm and Sydow's work [2018]), contractual governance is less effective, and needs to be complemented (or substituted) by relational governance arrangements. Thus, large portfolios with sparse relationships and redundant technical competence, where partners are similar in size and characteristics, tend to reduce contractual governance efficacy and to increase relational governance effectiveness (Dyer, 2000; Gulati & Sytch, 2007; MacDuffie & Helper, 1997).

When cooperation between partners prevails—as in the Toyota case described by Wilhelm and Sydow (2018), and synergies are effectively exploited also between focal firms' partners, both relational and contractual governance increase their effectiveness. As proposed by the authors, relational mechanisms are mostly used for coordination and joint problem solving, while contractual governance is introduced later in the development of the relationship when control is needed. In terms of portfolios' characteristics, small portfolios dense with relationships and characterized by complementary assets, where partners differ in terms of size and characteristics, relational and contractual governance are both effective (Gulati & Sytch, 2007) and, as suggested by Wilhelm and Sydow (2018), play a complementary role in governing IORs (Dyer, 2000; MacDuffie & Helper, 1997).

2.3.2 Exchange Hazards at the Focal-Firm Level from a Portfolio Perspective

Scholars exploring alliance portfolios noted that firms can learn about different ways to design and manage IORs that can then replicate across their relationships (Gulati, 1999; Gupta & Misra, 2000; Lyles & Lyles, 1988; Simonin, 1997). The two main sources of learning have been identified with the experience (Hoang & Rothaermel, 2005) and the collaborative know-how (Simonin, 1997) that focal firms accumulate through the development of several IORs—where particular emphasis has been placed on the number of different partners and the duration of the relationships (Sampson, 2005).

Consequently, when focal firms develop alliance portfolios that are diverse in terms of partners' characteristics, object of exchange, and governance arrangements, and that are constituted by long-term relationships, they will gain access to a broad repertoire of experiences that can lead to superior learning and capabilities in assessing and managing exchange hazards of present and future relationships. For example, thanks to their experience and collaborative know-how, firms can set-up internal processes to mitigate transaction-specific investments, and transfer inter-organizational knowledge (Powell et al., 1996) to promote learning within and across the alliance portfolio, as Toyota did with the development of knowledge-sharing routines across its relationships to promote superior learning in its entire supplier network (Dyer & Nobeoka, 2000).

However, as noted by previous literature, when firms engage with the governance of such complex relational structures, they will incur in higher transaction costs (Ozcan & Eisenhardt, 2009; Prashant & Harbir, 2009; Sarkar et al., 2009), resulting in complex coordination with and control of the different partners. A trade-off then exists between the opportunity of learning with whom to cooperate and how to cooperate, and the cost of coordinating large and diverse alliance portfolios (Sarkar et al., 2009).

However, this trade-off can have different valences depending on the type of governance mechanisms the firm is practicing with its partners. While relational governance refers to social norms that can be replicated across similar partnerships, contractual governance usually concerns tailored codified or uncodified (Keller et al., 2021) governance arrangements more formal in nature, and what is learnt in one context is not necessarily exported to another relationship (Hoetker & Mellewigt, 2009). In general, then, we can say that when alliance portfolios are large and diverse, the cost of managing the complex structure is counterbalanced if the firms are relying on relational governance, since what is learnt in some relationships, can be used and replicated in others. Conversely, when firms are relying on contractual governance, the costs of tailoring the arrangements for a large and diverse set of ties will be higher than the benefits deriving from accumulated knowledge and experience.

From the focal-firm point of view, when alliance portfolios are large and diverse, relational governance can be more effective for its higher value in terms of experience and collaborative know-how, while contractual governance is more valuable when the firm is managing alliance portfolios more homogeneous and of smaller size.

2.4 Governing Collaborations at the Whole Network Level

As stated by Granovetter (1992), "the fact that economic action and outcomes, like all social action and outcomes, are affected by actors' dyadic (pair wise) relations *and* by the structure of the overall network of relations" (Granovetter, 1992, p. 33) indicates that both dimensions must be taken into account to explain IORs exchanges. Pilbeam et al. (2012) noted that there is now substantial agreement on the fact that supply chains relationships are embedded in their supply networks, and that research should focus on the entire supply network rather than on interactions between isolated pairs of firms (Anderson et al., 1994; Choi et al.,

2001; Olsen & Ellram, 1997). This level of analysis has regained attention within the recent debate on embeddedness (Granovetter, 2017; Krippner et al., 2004; Moran, 2005), where scholars emphasized that in order to have a thorough understanding of the focal firm outcome it is necessary to analyze not only particular dyadic relations, "[...] but also the aggregated impact of all such relations." (Granovetter, 2017, p. 17). Past research stressed the importance of distinguishing the network level from the portfolio level, as for example in Doz and Hamel (1998) where the authors propose the term 'alliance web', defining it as "a set of alliances that are more interdependent than a portfolio" (Doz & Hamel, 1998, p. 223), or as in Lorenzoni and Baden-Fuller (1995) where the'web of alliances' is defined as a network led by a focal firm (Wassmer, 2010).

Overall, empirical research exploring alliance networks adopted two different perspectives: the network/industry-level of analysis (e.g., Gulati & Gargiulo, 1999; Schilling & Phelps, 2007), and the focal firm (egocentric) perspective (Powell et al., 1996). The former approach explored how different network's characteristics, such as network density (Krippner et al., 2004), strength of relationships (Uzzi, 1997), and the presence of structural holes (Burt, 1992, 2009) affect network's exchange hazards, affecting the relative effectiveness of governance mechanisms. The latter, focused on firm-level indicators describing how the firm is positioned within its network of relationships, such as focal-firm centrality (Gulati & Gargiulo, 1999) and brokerage (Burt, 2009), emphasizing how the value of different forms of governance can be contingent to these dimensions. Such variables, in fact, have been found to be related to inter-firm exchange hazards by research exploring how network structural features influence uncertainty and transaction-specific investments. Then, the discussion of these different structural dimensions contributes to answer to the question: *How does the value of governance mechanisms change depending on the firm's embeddedness and positioning within its network of IORs?*

2.4.1 Exchange Hazards at the Network Level

Network's features used to analyze the contingent value of governance mechanisms have been approached mainly from a structural perspective, relying on the social network analysis formalization. In order to understand how the network structure can influence exchange hazards between partners and, consequently, the effectiveness of formal and informal governance, three main dimensions will be discussed: network density (Kilduff & Tsai, 2003), the intensity of ties' strength (Granovetter, 1973), and the presence of structural holes (Burt, 1992).

Density. Density is used in Social Network Analysis as the measure of the ratio between actual ties over the number of all possible ties in a network, representing how much a network is dense with social connections between its members (Kilduff & Tsai, 2003). The density concept is also associated with the structural embeddedness of a network (Moran, 2005; Yang et al., 2011). The density of alliance networks favours the creation and the enforcement of social norms, or more general shared meanings, and reassures firms that the expensive and risky project will go as they expect, and that there will be no surprises from the other partners (Krippner et al., 2004). Density assumes also a geographical connotation in those studies exploring dense local clustering: in Schilling and Phelps (2007), for example, these type of alliance networks have been found fostering communication and cooperation, increasing innovative output of firms. Similar dynamics are those associated with industrial districts, in which firms cooperating within such a network are embedded into a social and business context where they share "the rules of the game" (Brusco, 1999), thus inhibiting opportunistic behaviours and increasing partners' cooperative attitude (Becattini, 1990; Farrell & Knight, 2003; Molina-Morales & Martinez-Fernandez, 2006; Whittington et al., 2009). In such contexts, relational governance is foundational of inter-organizational collaborations, which explicitly rely on handshakes and informal practices of coordination for developing joint projects thanks to the social context sustained by the wider alliance network (Cao & Lumineau, 2015; Uzzi, 1997; Yang et al., 2011). On the other hand, contractual governance results as ineffective when not detrimental for IORs performance, since the formal arrangement is seen as an unnecessary effort or a signal of mistrust (Brusco, 1999; Whitford, 2001; Yang et al., 2011).

Strength of relationships. Tightly related to network density is the concept of tie strength, which is associated with relational embeddedness, namely the qualification of a network's ties through a quality lens that identifies embedded/strong and arm's-length/weak ties (Granovetter, 1973, 1983; Uzzi, 1996, 1997). In fact, when a network is characterized by many strong ties its density will be higher, while the reverse is true for networks mainly characterized by weak ties (Granovetter, 1983). Following the Strength of Weak Ties (SWT) theory, a network characterized mainly by strong ties is a network where "new ideas will spread slowly, scientific endeavours will be handicapped, and subgroups separated by race, ethnicity, geography, or other characteristics will have difficulty reaching a modus vivendi" (Granovetter, 1983, p. 202). The theoretical proposal of the SWT is that strong relationships tend to encourage triadic closure, reducing the opportunity to access more vast external knowledge. However, strong ties have also greater motivation to cooperate, and are typically more easily available (Coleman, 1988). Moreover, within a network characterized by strong ties, we can expect transitivity (firm A has a strong tie with firm B, firm B is strongly connected to firm C, firm A and firm C will be likely connected by a strong tie too). In such networks, then, ties are mostly cooperative relationships, and the speed of flow, credibility, and influence are significant (Granovetter, 1983; Weimann, 1980). Strong ties increase the predictability of partners' behaviours (ruled by social norms, reciprocity, etc.) and, therefore, networks dense with strong ties result in lower exchange hazards (Burt, 2000). However, strong ties are relationships whose deep social nature requires to rely mainly on relational governance, being the costs of negotiating contracts wasteful and the 'handshake' between partners considered as more than sufficient (Zaheer & Venkatraman, 1995). On the other hand, weak ties are those relationships opening networks to other networks, working as bridges between different communities. In innovation contexts, accessing to novel ideas and complementary knowledge is essential for firms' results: weak ties are then a key driver for innovation, and networks dense with weak ties are more dynamic and innovation-intensive (Todo et al., 2016). However, being weak ties less embedded by definition, they increase the uncertainty of the network environment, and they require more transaction-specific investments, increasing the overall exchange hazards. Then, although diverse and sparse networks favour performance, when firms need to access external knowledge for developing distributed innovation, the partner's active cooperation is needed and thus governance mechanisms are key to exploit such opportunities (Granovetter, 1985): contractual governance will be effective in safeguarding against potential opportunistic behaviours of weak ties, and relational governance will effectively complement it improving the partners' behaviours predictability (Yang et al., 2011).

Structural holes. Structural holes are defined by Burt (1992) as the missing ties between disconnected parts of a network: they are relevant for the so-called Social Capital Theory that states that social capital (a metaphor for the advantage a subject can get thanks to its positioning within its network) is created by "a network in which people can broker connections between otherwise disconnected segments" (Burt, 2017, p. 31). Networks rich in structural holes are networks in which knowledge flows are controlled by few agents acting as brokers: knowledge and information flows are thus reduced, and (Phelps et al., 2012) the whole network is less dense in social relationships. As a consequence, exchange hazards are present, since uncertainty towards alters' behaviors is low only for brokers, and transactions-specific investments (especially towards brokers) are required. In such a context, contractual governance is effective in reassuring IORs' partners about potential opportunistic behaviors; however, in innovation contexts, relational governance will be necessary to repair for contracts' incompleteness.

2.4.2 Exchange Hazards at the Focal-Firm Level from a Network Perspective

The network perspective can be used also to explore what happens at the focal-firm level, somehow adding new features to the description of the firm under analysis related to its positioning within its network. Such features have been showed influencing (as the others discussed in the subsection 2.4.1) the contingent value of governance mechanisms since the firm's (structural) position within its network of relationship can influence the exchange hazards related to its IORs (Ahuja et al., 2009; Polidoro et al., 2011). In order to explore such contingencies, two main firms' characteristics—from a network perspective—will be analyzed: the focal-firm centrality (Polidoro et al., 2011) and its brokering position (Burt, 2000; Zaheer & Venkatraman, 1995).

Focal-firm centrality. When a firm is structurally embedded within its network of relationships, it is more likely to form new partnerships because of its opportunity to gather information about a large number of potential ties (Gulati, 1995), and because of its high status that a central position confers to the firm (Podolny, 1994). Centrality is thus a structural characteristic that offers unique opportunities to the central firm to exploit potential benefits deriving from its network of relationships (Polidoro et al., 2011), and providing extra information and knowledge due to the firm's social capital (Burt, 2004). In such a context, the firm is able to reduce at their minimum the uncertainty about its counterparts and the risk of being exploited, while gets the opportunity to exploit more peripheral counterparts. Similarly to the power asymmetry argument discussed in subsection 2.4.1, the reasoning about the contingent value of relational mechanisms can be extended also to the centrality attribute, where the central firm is the more powerful and the peripheral ones hold less power. More central firms will need relational governance to reassure more peripheral actors, even though from central firms' perspective it is less effective because it requires a lot of relational investments to create and maintain trust between the parties. On the other hand, contractual governance would be more effective for central firms, given they have more information about the whole network situation, but less effective for peripheral actors, who will fear that the information asymmetry will be at their detriment.

Brokerage. The brokerage dimension mirrors at the focal-firm level what has been described at the whole network level in terms of structural holes. The broker firm is the one occupying the network's structural hole, namely connecting otherwise disconnected segments. Thus, in other words, a firm able to fill a structural hole, occupies a very advantageous position because it will be the broker of relationships between the isolated groups: information, knowledge, and other kind of resources (Zaheer & Venkatraman, 1995) will flow from one side to the other of the network passing through the brokering organization that will be exposed to nonredundant information (Burt, 1992). Although the brokerage position favors the connecting firm's performance, in the innovation context the access to external knowledge requires the active cooperation of the partner (Granovetter, 1985). The broker firm occupies the network position that, by definition, lowers exchange hazards: it will have the lowest possible uncertainty about potential partners' behaviors because of its access to nonredundant information flows within the network, and given its key position it will be less exposed to potential opportunistic behaviors by its counterparts. In this situation, as previously commented, the contractual governance would be most effective. However, firms not occupying any structural holes, in order to provide the 'active cooperation' will need to increase the safeguards against the threat of being exploited by their alters: from their perspective, relational governance will be of higher value.

2.5 Concluding Remarks: The Contingent Value of Governance Mechanisms

In this chapter we provided additional insights on how successful collaborations for innovation may be achieved focusing on the contingent value of governance mechanisms in dyads, IORs portfolios, and networks. To explore such an issue, we relied on IORs literature that typically refers to the dichotomy between contractual and relational governance. Contractual governance, on the one side, provides specific recourse to the legal system, by defining enforceable penalties when expectations are not met that can, in turn, sustain cooperation by deterring opportunistic or exploitative behaviors (Li et al., 2010; Williamson, 1985). Relational norms refer to those social frameworks based on shared expectations that help transacting parties to mitigate opportunism and to coordinate, to flexibly adjust their expectations of each other in the face of unpredictable events (Achrol & Gundlach, 1999; Cannon et al., 2000; Dyer & Singh, 1998; Eckerd et al., 2021). We discussed how these different features of contractual and relational governance make them more or less valuable in different IORs, depending on the dyad, the portfolio, and the larger network within which relationships are embedded. What emerged from this review of the literature is that exchange hazards (uncertainty and transaction-specific investments) assume different intensity and nuances depending on the analytical level and the perspective (focal-firm vs. alters) adopted. What emerged consistently is that relational and contractual governance value is often polarized between the focal-firm and alters when asymmetries are in place: what is best for the one party, it is not preferable for the other. Moreover, this contingency is even more stressed if we shift from one level of analysis to the other: what could be valuable when looking at the individual firm, becomes less effective if considered at the portfolio level, or in terms of network structure.

The present chapter then helped to answer to the research question about whether the value of governance mechanisms is consistent between levels of analysis: the answer is negative, and the analysis uncovered only partially the different tensions and trade-offs that can emerge when firms need to define their governance strategy for IORs. However, the implication of this result is clear and points to the direction of relational capabilities: in such a complex and interdependent strategic domain, firms must develop specific competences and knowledge about how to cope with the contingent value of relational and contractual governance at the dyad, portfolio, and whole network levels of analysis. This matter will be explored in-depth in Chapter 3.

References

Abdi, M., & Aulakh, P. S. (2012). Do country-level institutional frameworks and interfirm governance arrangements substitute or complement in international business relationships? *Journal of International Business Studies, 43*, 477–497.

Abdi, M., & Aulakh, P. S. (2017). Locus of uncertainty and the relationship between contractual and relational governance in cross-border interfirm relationships. *Journal of Management, 43*(3), 771–803. https://doi.org/10.1177/0149206314541152

Achrol, R. S., & Gundlach, G. T. (1999). Legal and social safeguards against opportunism in exchange. *Journal of Retailing, 75*(1), 107–124.

Adler, P. S., Benner, M., Brunner, D. J., MacDuffie, J. P., Osono, E., Staats, B. R., Takeuchi, H., Tushman, M., & Winter, S. G. (2009). Perspectives on the productivity dilemma. *Journal of Operations Management, 27*(2), 99–113.

Ahuja, G. (2000). Collaboration networks, structural holes, and innovation: A longitudinal study. *Administrative Science Quarterly, 45*(3), 425–455. https://doi.org/10.2307/2667105

Ahuja, G., Polidoro, F., & Mitchell, W. (2009). Structural homophily or social asymmetry? The formation of alliances by poorly embedded firms. *Strategic Management Journal, 30*(9), 941–958.

Albers, S., Wohlgezogen, F., & Zajac, E. J. (2016). Strategic alliance structures: An organization design perspective. *Journal of Management, 42*(3), 582–614.

Anderson, E., & Weitz, B. (1989). Determinants of continuity in conventional industrial channel dyads. *Marketing Science, 8*(4), 310–323.

Anderson, J. C., Håkansson, H., & Johanson, J. (1994). Dyadic business relationships within a business network context. *Journal of Marketing, 58*(4), 1–15.

Anderson, J. C., & Narus, J. A. (1984). A model of the distributor's perspective of distributor-manufacturer working relationships. *Journal of Marketing, 48*(4), 62–74.

Azadegan, A. (2011). Benefiting from supplier operational innovativeness: The influence of supplier evaluations and absorptive capacity. *Journal of Supply Chain Management, 47*(2), 49–64.

Bae, J., & Gargiulo, M. (2004). Partner substitutability, alliance network structure, and firm profitability in the telecommunications industry. *Academy of Management Journal, 47*(6), 843–859. https://doi.org/10.5465/20159626

Baum, J. A. C., Calabrese, T., & Silverman, B. S. (2000). Don't go it alone: Alliance network composition and startups' performance in Canadian biotechnology. *Strategic Management Journal, 21*(3), 267–294. http://www.jstor.org/stable/3094188

Becattini, G. (1990). The Marshallian industrial district as a socio-economic notion. In F. Pyke, G. Becattini, & W. Sengenberger (Eds.), *Industrial districts and inter-firm co-operation in Italy* (pp. 37–51). International Institute for Labor Studies.

Brusco, S. (1999). The rules of the game in industrial districts. In A. Grandori (Ed.), *Interfirm networks: Organization and industrial competitiveness* (pp. 17–40). Routledge.

Burkert, M., Ivens, B. S., & Shan, J. (2012). Governance mechanisms in domestic and international buyer–supplier relationships: An empirical study. *Industrial Marketing Management, 41*(3), 544–556. https://doi.org/10.1016/j.indmarman.2011.06.019

Burt, R. S. (1992). *Structural holes: The social structure of competition*. Harvard University Press.

Burt, R. S. (1997). The contingent value of social capital. *Administrative Science Quarterly, 42*(2), 339–365. https://doi.org/10.2307/2393923

Burt, R. S. (2000). The network structure of social capital. *Research in Organizational Behavior, 22*, 345–423.

Burt, R. S. (2004). Structural holes and good ideas. *American Journal of Sociology, 110*(2), 349–399. https://doi.org/10.1086/421787

Burt, R. S. (2009). *Structural holes: The social structure of competition*. Harvard University Press.

Burt, R. S. (2017). Structural holes versus network closure as social capital. In *Social capital* (pp. 31–56). Routdledge.

Cai, S., Jun, M., & Yang, Z. (2010). Implementing supply chain information integration in China: The role of institutional forces and trust. *Journal of Operations Management, 28*(3), 257–268. https://doi.org/10.1016/j.jom.2009.11.005

Cannon, J. P., Achrol, R. S., & Gundlach, G. T. (2000). Contracts, norms, and plural form governance. *Journal of the Academy of Marketing Science, 28*(2), 180. https://doi.org/10.1177/0092070300282001

Cao, Z., & Lumineau, F. (2015). Revisiting the interplay between contractual and relational governance: A qualitative and meta-analytic investigation. *Journal of Operations Management, 33*, 15–42.

Choi, T. Y., Dooley, K. J., & Rungtusanatham, M. (2001). Supply networks and complex adaptive systems: Control versus emergence. *Journal of Operations Management, 19*(3), 351–366.

Claycomb, C., & Frankwick, G. L. (2004). A contingency perspective of communication, conflict resolution and buyer search effort in buyer-supplier relationships. *Journal of Supply Chain Management, 40*(4), 18–34.

Coleman, J. S. (1988). Social capital in the creation of human capital. *American Journal of Sociology, 94*, 95–120.

Crook, T. R., & Combs, J. G. (2007). Sources and consequences of bargaining power in supply chains. *Journal of Operations Management, 25*(2), 546–555.

Dahl, R. A. (2005). *Who governs?: Democracy and power in an American city*. Yale University Press.

Dore, R. (1983). Goodwill and the spirit of market capitalism. *The British Journal of Sociology, 34*(4), 459–482. http://www.jstor.org/stable/590932

Doz, Y. L., & Hamel, G. (1998). *Alliance advantage: The art of creating value through partnering*. Harvard Business Press.

Dyer, J. H. (1997). Effective interim collaboration: How firms minimize transaction costs and maximise transaction value. *Strategic Management Journal, 18*(7), 535–556. https://doi.org/10.1002/(SICI)1097-0266(199708)18:7%3c535::AID-SMJ885%3e3.0.CO;2-Z

Dyer, J. H. (2000). *Collaborative advantage: Winning through extended enterprise supply networks*. Oxford University Press.

Dyer, J. H., & Nobeoka, K. (2000). Creating and managing a high-performance knowledge-sharing network: The Toyota case. *Strategic Management Journal, 21*(3), 345–367.

Dyer, J. H., & Singh, H. (1998). The relational view: Cooperative strategy and sources of interorganizational competitive advantage. *The Academy of Management Review, 23*(4), 660–679. http://www.jstor.org/stable/259056

Eckerd, S., Handley, S., & Lumineau, F. (2021). Trust violations in buyer-supplier relationships: Spillovers and the contingent role of governance structures. *Journal of Supply Chain Management, n/a*(n/a). https://doi.org/10.1111/jscm.12270

Emerson, R. M. (1981). Social exchange theory. In M. Rosenberg & R. H. Turner (Eds.), *Social psychology: Sociological perspectives*. Transaction Publishers.

Esper, T. L., Ellinger, A. E., Stank, T. P., Flint, D. J., & Moon, M. (2010). Demand and supply integration: A conceptual framework of value creation through knowledge management. *Journal of the Academy of Marketing Science, 38*, 5–18.

Farrell, H., & Knight, J. (2003). Trust, institutions, and institutional change: Industrial districts and the social capital hypothesis. *Politics & Society, 31*(4), 537–566. https://doi.org/10.1177/0032329203256954

Fryxell, G. E., Dooley, R. S., & Vryza, M. (2002). After the ink dries: The interaction of trust and control in US-based international joint ventures. *Journal of Management Studies, 39*(6), 865–886.

Gargiulo, M., & Benassi, M. (2000). Trapped in your own net? Network cohesion, structural holes, and the adaptation of social capital. *Organization Science, 11*(2), 183–196. https://doi.org/10.2307/2640283

George, G., Zahra, S. A., Wheatley, K. K., & Khan, R. (2001). The effects of alliance portfolio characteristics and absorptive capacity on performance: A study of biotechnology firms. *The Journal of High Technology Management Research, 12*(2), 205–226. https://doi.org/10.1016/S1047-8310(01)00037-2

Gilson, R. J., Sabel, C. F., & Scott, R. E. (2009). Contracting for innovation: Vertical disintegration and interfirm collaboration. *Columbia Law Review, 109*(3), 431–502.

Graebner, M. E., Lumineau, F., & Fudge Kamal, D. (2020). Unrequited: Asymmetry in interorganizational trust. *Strategic Organization, 18*(2), 362–374.

Granovetter, M. (1973). The strength of weak ties. *American Journal of Sociology, 78*(6), 1360–1380. http://www.jstor.org/stable/2776392

Granovetter, M. (1983). The strength of weak ties: A network theory revisited. *Sociological Theory, 1*, 201–233.

Granovetter, M. (1985). Economic action and social structure: The problem of embeddedness. *American Journal of Sociology, 91*(3), 481–510.

Granovetter, M. (1992). Economic institutions as social constructions: A framework for analysis. *Acta Sociologica, 35*(1), 3–11. http://www.jstor.org/stable/4194749

Granovetter, M. (2017). *Society and economy: Framework and principles*. Harvard University Press.

Gulati, R. (1995). Social structure and alliance formation patterns: A longitudinal analysis. *Administrative Science Quarterly, 40*(4), 619–652. http://www.jstor.org/stable/2393756

Gulati, R. (1998). Alliances and networks. *Strategic Management Journal, 19*(4), 293–317.

Gulati, R. (1999). Network location and learning: The influence of network resources and firm capabilities on alliance formation. *Strategic Management Journal, 20*(5), 397–420.

Gulati, R., & Gargiulo, M. (1999). Where do interorganizational networks come from? *American Journal of Sociology, 104*(5), 1439–1493. https://doi.org/10.1086/210179

Gulati, R., Lavie, D., & Madhavan, R. (2011). How do networks matter? The performance effects of interorganizational networks. *Research in Organizational Behavior, 31*, 207–224. https://doi.org/10.1016/j.riob.2011.09.005

Gulati, R., & Sytch, M. (2007). Dependence asymmetry and joint dependence in interorganizational relationships: Effects of embeddedness on a manufacturer's performance in procurement relationships. *Administrative Science Quarterly, 52*(1), 32–69.

Gulati, R., & Zajac, E. J. (1998). Commentary on 'alliances and networks' by R. Gulati. *Strategic Management Journal*, 319–321.

Gupta, A., & Misra, L. (2000). The value of experiential learning by organizations: Evidence from international joint ventures. *Journal of Financial Research, 23*(1), 77–102.

Gupta, A. K., Smith, K. G., & Shalley, C. E. (2006). The interplay between exploration and exploitation. *Academy of Management Journal, 49*(4), 693–706.

Hausman, A., & Johnston, W. J. (2010). The impact of coercive and non-coercive forms of influence on trust, commitment, and compliance in supply chains. *Industrial Marketing Management, 39*(3), 519–526.

Heide, J. B., & John, G. (1990). Alliances in industrial purchasing: The determinants of joint action in buyer-supplier relationships. *Journal of Marketing Research, 27*(1), 24–36. https://doi.org/10.1177/002224379002700103

Helper, S., MacDuffie, J., & Sabel, C. F. (2000). Pragmatic collaborations: Advancing knowledge while controlling opportunism. *Industrial and Corporate Change, 9*(3), 443–488.

Hingley, M. K. (2005). Power to all our friends? Living with imbalance in supplier–retailer relationships. *Industrial Marketing Management, 34*(8), 848–858.

Hoang, H., & Rothaermel, F. T. (2005). The effect of general and partner-specific alliance experience on joint R&D project performance. *Academy of Management Journal, 48*(2), 332–345.

Hoetker, G., & Mellewigt, T. (2009). Choice and performance of governance mechanisms: Matching alliance governance to asset type. *Strategic Management Journal, 30*(10), 1025–1044. https://doi.org/10.1002/smj.775

Hoffmann, W. H. (2007). Strategies for managing a portfolio of alliances. *Strategic Management Journal, 28*(8), 827–856. https://doi.org/10.1002/smj.607

Howard, M., Roehrich, J. K., Lewis, M. A., & Squire, B. (2019). Converging and diverging governance mechanisms: The role of (dys)function in long-term inter-organizational relationships. *British Journal of Management, 30*(3), 624–644. https://doi.org/10.1111/1467-8551.12254

Hult, G. T. M., Ketchen, D. J., & Arrfelt, M. (2007). Strategic supply chain management: Improving performance through a culture of competitiveness and knowledge development. *Strategic Management Journal, 28*(10), 1035–1052.

Johnsen, R. E., & Ford, D. (2008). Exploring the concept of asymmetry: A typology for analysing customer–supplier relationships. *Industrial Marketing Management, 37*(4), 471–483. https://doi.org/10.1016/j.indmarman.2007.05.004

Keller, A., Lumineau, F., Mellewigt, T., & Ariño, A. (2021). Alliance governance mechanisms in the face of disruption. *Organization Science, 32*(6), 1542–1570. https://doi.org/10.1287/orsc.2021.1437

Kilduff, M., & Tsai, W. (2003). *Social networks and organizations*. SAGE Publications Ltd. https://doi.org/10.4135/9781849209915

Krippner, G. R., Granovetter, M., Block, F., Biggart, N., Beamish, T., Hsing, Y., Hart, G., Arrighi, G., Mendell, M., Hall, J., Burawoy, M., Vogel, S., & O'Rian, S. (2004). Polanyi symposium: A conversation on embeddedness. *Socio-Economic Review, 2*, 109–135.

Kumar, N., Scheer, L. K., & Steenkamp, J.-B.E.M. (1995). The effects of supplier fairness on vulnerable resellers. *Journal of Marketing Research, 32*(1), 54–65. https://doi.org/10.2307/3152110

Lavie, D. (2006). The competitive advantage of interconnected firms: An extension of the resource-based view. *The Academy of Management Review, 31*(3), 638–658. http://www.jstor.org/stable/20159233

Lavie, D. (2007). Alliance portfolios and firm performance: A study of value creation and appropriation in the U.S. software industry. *Strategic Management Journal, 28*(12), 1187–1212. https://doi.org/10.1002/smj.637

Lee, C.-J., & Johnsen, R. E. (2012). Asymmetric customer–supplier relationship development in Taiwanese electronics firms. *Industrial Marketing Management, 41*(4), 692–705. https://doi.org/10.1016/j.indmarman.2011.09.017

Li, Y., Xie, E., Teo, H.-H., & Peng, M. W. (2010). Formal control and social control in domestic and international buyer–supplier relationships. *Journal of operations management, 28*(4), 333–344. https://doi.org/10.1016/j.jom.2009.11.008

Lorenzoni, G., & Baden-Fuller, C. (1995). Creating a strategic center to manage a web of partners. *California Management Review, 37*(3), 146–163.

Lumineau, F. (2017). How contracts influence trust and distrust. *Journal of Management, 43*(5), 1553–1577. https://doi.org/10.1177/0149206314556656

Lumineau, F., & Henderson, J. E. (2012). The influence of relational experience and contractual governance on the negotiation strategy in buyer–supplier disputes. *Journal of Operations Management, 30*(5), 382–395.

Lumineau, F., Jin, J. L., Sheng, S., & Zhou, K. Z. (2022). Asset specificity asymmetry and supplier opportunism in buyer–supplier exchanges. *Journal of Business Research, 149*, 85–100. https://doi.org/10.1016/j.jbusres.2022.05.011

Lumineau, F., & Oliveira, N. (2018). A pluralistic perspective to overcome major blind spots in research on interorganizational relationships. *Academy of Management Annals, 12*(1), 440–465.

Luo, Y. (2005). How important are shared perceptions of procedural justice in cooperative alliances? *Academy of Management Journal, 48*(4), 695–709.

Lyles, M. A., & Lyles, M. A. (1988). Learning among joint-venture sophisticated firms. *Management International Review*, Special Issue.

MacDuffie, J. P., & Helper, S. (1997). Creating lean suppliers: Diffusing lean production through the supply chain. *California Management Review, 39*(4), 118–151.

MacDuffie, J. P., & Helper, S. (2007). Collaboration in supply chains: With and without trust. In C. Heckscher & P. Adler (Eds.), *The firm as a collaborative community* (pp. 417–466). Oxford University Press.

Malhotra, D., & Lumineau, F. (2011). Trust and collaboration in the aftermath of conflict: The effects of contract structure. *Academy of Management Journal, 54*(5), 981–998.

Mayer, K. J., & Argyres, N. S. (2004). Learning to contract: Evidence from the personal computer industry. *Organization Science, 15*(4), 394–410.

Mayer, R. C., Davis, J. H., & Schoorman, F. D. (1995). An integrative model of organizational trust. *Academy of Management Review, 20*(3), 709–734.

Molina-Morales, F. X., & Martinez-Fernandez, M. T. (2006). Industrial districts: Something more than a neighbourhood. *Entrepreneurship and Regional Development, 18*(November), 503–524.

Moran, P. (2005). Structural vs. Relational embeddedness: Social capital and managerial performance. *Strategic Management Journal, 26*(12), 1129–1151. http://www.jstor.org/stable/20142298

Moriarty, R. T., Jr., & Spekman, R. E. (1984). An empirical investigation of the information sources used during the industrial buying process. *Journal of Marketing Research, 21*(2), 137–147.

Noordewier, T. G., John, G., & Nevin, J. R. (1990). Performance outcomes of purchasing arrangements in industrial buyer-vendor relationships. *Journal of Marketing, 54*(4), 80–93.

Nooteboom, B., Berger, H., & Noorderhaven, N. G. (1997). Effects of trust and governance on relational risk. *Academy of Management Journal, 40*(2), 308–338. https://doi.org/10.2307/256885

Nyaga, G. N., Lynch, D. F., Marshall, D., & Ambrose, E. (2013). Power asymmetry, adaptation and collaboration in dyadic relationships involving a powerful partner. *Journal of Supply Chain Management, 49*(3), 42–65.

Oliver, C. (1990). Determinants of interorganizational relationships: Integration and future directions. *Academy of Management Review, 15*(2), 241–265. https://doi.org/10.5465/amr.1990.4308156

Olsen, R. F., & Ellram, L. M. (1997). Buyer-supplier relationships: Alternative research approaches. *European Journal of Purchasing & Supply Management, 3*(4), 221–231.

Oxley, J. E. (1997). Appropriability hazards and governance in strategic alliances: A transaction cost approach. *The Journal of Law, Economics, and Organization, 13*(2), 387–409.

Ozcan, P., & Eisenhardt, K. M. (2009). Origin of alliance portfolios: Entrepreneurs, network strategies, and firm performance [case study]. *Academy of Management Journal, 52*, 246–279. https://doi.org/10.5465/amj.2009.37308021

Park, S. H., & Zhou, D. (2005). Firm heterogeneity and competitive dynamics in alliance formation. *Academy of Management Review, 30*(3), 531–554.

Phelps, C., Heidl, R., & Wadhwa, A. (2012). Knowledge, networks, and knowledge networks: A review and research agenda. *Journal of Management, 38*(4), 1115–1166. https://doi.org/10.1177/0149206311432640

Pilbeam, C., Alvarez, G., & Wilson, H. (2012). The governance of supply networks: A systematic literature review. *Supply Chain Management: An International Journal, 17*(4), 358–376. https://doi.org/10.1108/13598541211246512

Pisano, G. P. (1989). Using equity participation to support exchange: Evidence from the biotechnology industry. *The Journal of Law, Economics, and Organization, 5*(1), 109–126.

Podolny, J. M. (1994). Market uncertainty and the social character of economic exchange. *Administrative Science Quarterly, 39*(3), 458–483.

Polidoro, F., Ahuja, G., & Mitchell, W. (2011). When the social structure overshadows competitive incentives: The effects of network embeddedness on joint venture dissolution. *Academy of Management Journal, 54*(1), 203–223.

Poppo, L., & Zenger, T. (2002). Do formal contracts and relational governance function as substitutes or complements? *Strategic Management Journal, 23*(8), 707–725. https://doi.org/10.1002/smj.249

Powell, W. W., Koput, K. W., & Smith-Doerr, L. (1996). Interorganizational collaboration and the locus of innovation: Networks of learning in biotechnology. *Administrative Science Quarterly, 41*(1), 116–145. http://www.jstor.org/stable/2393988

Prashant, K., & Harbir, S. (2009). Managing strategic alliances: What do we know now, and where do we go from here? *Academy of Management Perspectives, 23*(3), 45–62. https://doi.org/10.5465/amp.2009.43479263

Reuer, J. J., & Ariño, A. (2002). Contractual renegotiations in strategic alliances. *Journal of Management, 28*(1), 47–68.

Rindfleisch, A. (2000). Organizational trust and interfirm cooperation: An examination of horizontal versus vertical alliances. *Marketing Letters, 11*(1), 81–95. http://www.jstor.org/stable/40216560

Rousseau, D. M., Sitkin, S. B., Burt, R. S., & Camerer, C. (1998). Not so different after all: A cross-discipline view of trust. *Academy of Management Review, 23*(3), 393–404. https://doi.org/10.5465/amr.1998.926617

Rowley, T., Behrens, D., & Krackhardt, D. (2000). Redundant governance structures: An analysis of structural and relational embeddedness in the steel and semiconductor industries. *Strategic Management Journal, 21*(3), 369–386.

Sampson, R. C. (2005). Experience effects and collaborative returns in R&D alliances. *Strategic Management Journal, 26*(11), 1009–1031.

Sanders, N. R. (2008). Pattern of information technology use: The impact on buyer–supplier coordination and performance. *Journal of Operations Management, 26*(3), 349–367. https://doi.org/10.1016/j.jom.2007.07.003

Sarkar, M. B., Aulakh, P. S., & Madhok, A. (2009). Process capabilities and value generation in alliance portfolios. *Organization Science, 20*(3), 583–600. https://doi.org/10.1287/orsc.1080.0390

Schilling, M. A., & Phelps, C. C. (2007). Interfirm collaboration networks: The impact of large-scale network structure on firm innovation. *Management Science, 53*(7), 1113–1126.

Shipilov, A., Gulati, R., Kilduff, M., Li, S., & Tsai, W. (2014). Relational pluralism within and between organizations. *Academy of Management Journal, 57*(2), 449–459. https://doi.org/10.5465/amj.2013.1145

Simonin, B. L. (1997). The importance of collaborative know-how: An empirical test of the learning organization. *Academy of Management Journal, 40*(5), 1150–1174.

Srikanth, K., & Puranam, P. (2011). Integrating distributed work: Comparing task design, communication, and tacit coordination mechanisms. *Strategic Management Journal, 32*(8), 849–875.

Stuart, T. E. (2000). Interorganizational alliances and the performance of firms: A study of growth and innovation rates in a high-technology industry. *Strategic Management Journal, 21*(8), 791–811. http://www.jstor.org/stable/3094397

Sytch, M., & Tatarynowicz, A. (2014). Friends and foes: The dynamics of dual social structures. *Academy of Management Journal, 57*(2), 585–613.

Terpend, R., & Ashenbaum, B. (2012). The intersection of power, trust and supplier network size: Implications for supplier performance. *Journal of Supply Chain Management, 48*(3), 52–77.

Todo, Y., Matous, P., & Inoue, H. (2016). The strength of long ties and the weakness of strong ties: Knowledge diffusion through supply chain networks. *Research Policy, 45*(9), 1890–1906. https://doi.org/10.1016/j.respol.2016.06.008

Uzzi, B. (1996). The sources and consequences of embeddedness for the economic performance of organizations: The network effect. *American Sociological Review, 61*(4), 674–698.

Uzzi, B. (1997). Social structure and competition in interfirm networks: The paradox of embeddedness. *Administrative Science Quarterly, 42*(1), 35–67. http://www.jstor.org/stable/2393808

Vassolo, R. S., Anand, J., & Folta, T. B. (2004). Non-additivity in portfolios of exploration activities: A real options-based analysis of equity alliances in biotechnology. *Strategic Management Journal*, 25(11), 1045–1061.

Villena, V. H., Choi, T. Y., & Revilla, E. (2021). Mitigating mechanisms for the dark side of collaborative buyer–supplier relationships: A mixed-method study. *Journal of Supply Chain Management*, n/a(n/a). https://doi.org/10.1111/jscm.12239

Villena, V. H., & Craighead, C. W. (2017). On the same page? How asymmetric buyer–supplier relationships affect opportunism and performance. *Production and Operations Management*, 26(3), 491–508. https://doi.org/10.1111/poms.12648

Villena, V. H., Revilla, E., & Choi, T. Y. (2011). The dark side of buyer–supplier relationships: A social capital perspective. *Journal of Operations Management*, 29(6), 561–576. https://doi.org/10.1016/j.jom.2010.09.001

von Hippel, E. (1988). *The sources of innovation*. Oxford University Press.

Wagner, S. M., & Bode, C. (2014). Supplier relationship-specific investments and the role of safeguards for supplier innovation sharing. *Journal of Operations Management*, 32(3), 65–78. https://doi.org/10.1016/j.jom.2013.11.001

Wassmer, U. (2010). Alliance portfolios: A review and research agenda. *Journal of Management*, 36(1), 141–171. https://doi.org/10.1177/0149206308328484

Weber, L., & Mayer, K. (2014). Transaction cost economics and the cognitive perspective: Investigating the sources and governance of interpretive uncertainty. *Academy of Management Review*, 39(3), 344–363. https://doi.org/10.5465/amr.2011.0463

Weimann, G. (1980). *Conversation networks as communication networks* [Abstract of Ph. D. dissertation, University of Haifa].

Whitford, J. (2001). The decline of a model? Challenge and response in the Italian industrial districts. *Economy and Society*, 30(1), 38–65. https://doi.org/10.1080/03085140020019089

Whittington, K. B., Owen-Smith, J., & Powell, W. W. (2009). Networks, propinquity, and innovation in knowledge-intensive industries. *Administrative Science Quarterly*, 54(1), 90–122. https://doi.org/10.2189/asqu.2009.54.1.90

Wilhelm, M., & Sydow, J. (2018). Managing coopetition in supplier networks—A paradox perspective. *Journal of Supply Chain Management*, 54(3), 22–41. https://doi.org/10.1111/jscm.12167

Williamson, O. E. (1975). *Markets and hierarchies: Analysis and antitrust implications*. Free Press.

Williamson, O. E. (1979). Transaction-cost economics: The governance of contractual relations. *Journal of Law and Economics*, 22(2), 29. http://www.jstor.org/stable/725118

Williamson, O. E. (1985). *The economic institutions of capitalism*. Free Press.
Williamson, O. E. (1991). Comparative economic organization: The analysis of discrete structural alternatives. *Administrative Science Quarterly, 36*(2), 269–296. http://www.jstor.org/stable/2393356
Williamson, O. E. (1996). *The mechanisms of governance*. Oxford University Press.
Yang, Z., Zhou, C., & Jiang, L. (2011). When do formal control and trust matter? A context-based analysis of the effects on marketing channel relationships in China. *Industrial Marketing Management, 40*(1), 86–96. https://doi.org/10.1016/j.indmarman.2010.09.013
Zaheer, A., McEvily, B., & Perrone, V. (1998). Does trust matter? Exploring the effects of interorganizational and interpersonal trust on performance. *Organization Science, 9*(2), 141–159. http://www.jstor.org/stable/2640350
Zaheer, A., & Venkatraman, N. (1995). Relational governance as an interorganizational strategy: An empirical test of the role of trust in economic exchange. *Strategic Management Journal, 16*(5), 373–392. https://doi.org/10.1002/smj.4250160504
Zhao, H., Luo, Y., & Suh, T. (2004). Transaction cost determinants and ownership-based entry mode choice: A meta-analytical review. *Journal of International Business Studies, 35*, 524–544.

CHAPTER 3

Dynamics of Governance Mechanisms in Interorganizational Relationships

Abstract This chapter examines the dynamics of governance mechanisms in interorganizational relationships (IORs) and their adaptation in the face of disruptions. It contributes to the existing literature by exploring the contingent value and efficacy of different governance modes in sustaining collaboration and achieving desired outcomes. It begins with a review of literature on governance mechanisms in IORs, identifying gaps and emphasizing the need for investigating their dynamics. It then explores the factors and processes driving the evolution and adaptation of governance mechanisms during disruptions, highlighting the value of replicating mechanisms, leveraging knowledge, adapting competencies, and asserting power. The contingent value and limitations of replicating governance approaches are discussed. The chapter concludes by summarizing key insights and discussing implications for research and practice, emphasizing the importance of studying governance mechanism dynamics in managing disruptions in IORs.

Keywords Governance dynamics · Managing disruptions · Evolution of governance mechanisms · Adaptation · Replication

© The Author(s), under exclusive license to Springer Nature Switzerland AG 2024
S. Li Pira and A. Moretti, *Governing Interorganizational Relationships for Innovation*,
https://doi.org/10.1007/978-3-031-50229-3_3

3.1 Introduction

Interorganizational relationships (IORs) have emerged as the predominant form of collaboration among firms seeking to manage complex collaborative projects (Zollo et al., 2002). However, the inherent complexity and instability within these collaborations often present challenges that hinder partners from sustaining them over time (Keller et al., 2021). Recognizing this risk, the governance mechanisms employed in IORs play a pivotal role in addressing problems of cooperation and coordination among partners. Disruptions, as articulated in Chapter 1, encompass a range of unexpected shocks or alterations in the environment. These may manifest as technological advancements, shifts in customer preferences, or regulatory changes that possess the potential to profoundly influence the competitive landscape, diminishing the relevance or obsolescence of existing competencies. As disruptions occur, the nature and magnitude of cooperation and coordination problems may evolve, necessitating a reassessment of the effectiveness of governance mechanisms. Through an exploration of these mechanisms' dynamics, researchers and practitioners can gain invaluable insights into their adaptability and optimization, enabling the effective management of disruptions and ensuring the continued success of IORs. Understanding the dynamics of governance mechanisms is essential for comprehending their role in addressing cooperation and coordination challenges within IORs. Moreover, it offers insights into how the value of different governance mechanisms may transform when disruptions impact an IOR, empowering informed decision-making and facilitating adjustments to uphold effective collaboration.

Previous studies have examined alternative governance mechanisms, focusing on either structural (or contractual) approaches (Poppo & Zhou, 2014; Reuer & Ariño, 2007; Schepker et al., 2014) or relational governance mechanisms (Das & Teng, 1998; Schilke & Cook, 2013; Zaheer et al., 1998) in IORs. These perspectives have been explored both individually and in conjunction. However, while investigations into their complementarities have underscored their development through ongoing interactive practices, the dynamics elucidating the contingent value of these governance mechanisms remain elusive (Faems et al., 2008; Keller et al., 2021; Mayer & Argyres, 2004).

In this chapter, we delve into the dynamics of governance mechanisms in IORs, examining their evolution and adaptation in response to disrupting forces. These forces, including unexpected technological advancements, shifting customer preferences, and new regulations, introduce turbulence and uncertainty into the environment. Our aim is to illuminate the contingent value and efficacy of different governance modes in the face of such disruptions. This exploration yields valuable insights into the strategic choices firms make to sustain collaboration and goal achievement amidst industry transformation. Our analysis aims to deepen theoretical understanding of IORs governance dynamics under conditions of disruption.

The chapter's structure is as follows. Firstly, we provide an exhaustive review of existing literature on governance mechanisms in IORs, comprehensively examining both structural and relational perspectives. By identifying gaps in the current knowledge, we emphasize the need to investigate the dynamics and contingent value of these mechanisms.

Subsequently, we embark on an exploration of the dynamics of governance mechanisms, delving into the factors and processes that drive their adaptation and evolution when disruptions arise. We examine various theoretical approaches to elucidate the dynamics of governance mechanisms, highlighting the value of replicating these mechanisms across relationships to address similar complexities, leverage knowledge and insights, adapt established competencies to new contexts, and assert power and control. Additionally, we analyse the contingent value and efficacy of different governance modes across relationships, cautioning against the potential limitations of routinizing governance approaches that may impede adaptability and hinder firms' readiness for change, particularly in innovation projects.

Lastly, we conclude the chapter by summarizing key insights and discussing their implications for both research and practice. We emphasize the significance of studying the dynamics of governance mechanisms and the value it brings to understanding and managing disruptions within IORs.

In summary, this chapter presents a comprehensive examination of the dynamics of governance mechanisms in IORs. By investigating their adaptation and contingent value in the face of disruptions, we contribute to the existing literature on interorganizational collaboration, while offering practical insights to organizations engaged in IORs. Governance mechanisms play a crucial role in managing IORs, but the conceptual labels and classifications of these mechanisms in the literature have led to discrepancies and diverse perspectives (see Chapter 1). This chapter, building on the typology of governance mechanisms proposed in Chapter 1, sheds light on their dynamics, evolution, and interplay within IORs.

3.2 Evolution and Adaptation of Governance Mechanisms in Response to Shifting Interorganizational Relationships Under Disruption

In this section, we explore how governance mechanisms within interorganizational relationships evolve over time as partnerships undergo changes, particularly those brought on by disruptive forces. The development and adaptation of governance mechanisms pose a significant challenge, as the processes driving their evolution may differ from those influencing their initial design and implementation. This complexity is heightened amidst industry disruption, which prompts shifts in firm strategy and necessitates new governance approaches. As problems and knowledge needs change under uncertainty, firms must identify relevant partners and establish governance mechanisms that align to evolving search processes (Nickerson & Zenger, 2004). Thus, governance choices become interdependent with the development and safeguarding of knowledge and technology across partnerships. As firms encounter new problems due to disruption, they are compelled to modify their positioning and explore unfamiliar landscapes. Tracing how governance mechanisms are reconfigured and implemented through this strategic adaptation provides valuable insights. We analyse this evolution through several explanatory lenses: the problem-solving approach, the experiential learning approach, the evolutionary approach, and the political approach, which we will explore and analyse in detail throughout this section.

3.2.1 Problem Solving Approach to Governance of IORs

The governance mechanisms may adapt through problem-solving. Firms, operating in dynamic environments, must continuously analyse, interpret, and respond to the challenges they encounter (Cyert & March, 1963). The knowledge and experience acquired through problem-solving processes, subsequently shapes their future decisions and actions guiding firm's desire to find satisfactory solutions. The complexity of a problem plays a crucial role in determining the most effective method of searching for a solution and the importance of matching governance alternatives to problems based on their associated benefits and costs in governing solution search (Nickerson & Zenger, 2004).

A key assumption underlying this perspective is that the objective of a firm is to create valuable new knowledge. However, firms cannot simply choose the desired knowledge to acquire, as it often does not exist. Instead, they should focus on selecting valuable problems—those that, if successfully solved, would yield desirable knowledge or capability. Once a problem is identified, firms must then organize a search for solutions that maximizes the likelihood, speed, and cost-effectiveness of discovering valuable solutions matching appropriate governance mechanisms (Nickerson & Zenger, 2004).

Specifically, firms need to determine how to access relevant knowledge, either from within the organization or from external sources. However, while looking at the type of governance solutions might answer to the question of what forms of governance the firms implement, the challenge remains to understand the knowledge base of a firm leading to a set of capabilities that enhances the chances of growth and survival (Kogut & Zander, 1992).

In our view the firms' central competitive dimension is to adjust the governance mechanisms to the specific context. Adopting a problem-solving approach allows us to explain the adaptation of governance mechanisms as a quest for new alternatives, means to reduce slack, or methods to modify targets. This approach perceives firms as thoughtful entities, subject to cognitive errors and biases that can influence the proposed solutions (Weick, 1976). However, rather than just focusing on the transaction and how opportunism may drive the decision of which governance mechanisms to employ, our focus on the interorganizational processes show how the value of different governance types may vary depending on the role frames and heuristics developed within the firm and their influence on the choice of governance mechanisms (Foss & Weber, 2016) and the internal and external environment in which they are utilized.

For example, during the ideation phase, the rules that govern exchanges may not allow for a precise formulation of the aim and scope of a collaboration. In such a situation, a mechanism that does not require a detailed definition of the content of the exchange might be preferred. It is important to note that each perspective has its own set of challenges, particularly regarding the cognitive distinctiveness of organizations, which introduces the risk of biases or errors in decision-making.

By adopting a problem-solving perspective, we gain insights into the role of interorganizational governance mechanisms in facilitating effective problem solving and knowledge creation. Understanding the fit between governance alternatives and problem complexity can contribute to the development of more robust and adaptive governance arrangements that enhance interorganizational collaboration and improve organizational outcomes.

3.2.2 Experiential Learning Approach to Governance of IORs

The organizational learning perspective offers valuable insights into the development of interorganizational governance mechanisms, particularly in relation to changes observed in their structure. Indeed, the experiential learning perspective highlights the incremental and local nature of the learning process between firms (Mayer & Argyres, 2004).

The experiential learning refers to the process through which firms acquire, interpret, and apply knowledge to improve their performance and adapt to their environment. When applied to interorganizational governance mechanisms, this perspective emphasizes the importance of learning not only at the firm level but also at the interorganizational level. In other words, the firms involved in a collaborative relationship engage in collective learning processes that shape the development of governance mechanisms.

The changes in the structure of interorganizational governance mechanisms, as suggested by the experiential learning perspective, go beyond what can be fully explained by changes in the assets at risk in the relationship. Instead, these changes can be largely attributed to learning processes in which the firms learn how to effectively work together, including the process of learning how to contract with each other.

The nature of this learning process, as indicated by the incremental and local nature of the experiential learning perspective, aligns with the organizational learning perspective. Organizations tend to learn through iterative cycles of action, reflection, and adjustment. As firms engage in collaborative activities and interact with one another, they accumulate knowledge and insights about the most effective ways to organize and govern their relationship.

This learning process involves a combination of explicit and tacit knowledge acquisition. Explicit knowledge refers to codified information that can be easily articulated and shared, such as documented procedures or formal contracts. Tacit knowledge, on the other hand, is more embedded in individuals' experiences, skills, and intuitive understandings. Tacit knowledge is often difficult to articulate and transfer explicitly, but it plays a crucial role in shaping how firms work together and design their governance mechanisms.

The learning perspective emphasizes that learning in interorganizational relationships is a dynamic and ongoing process. It involves not only the acquisition of new knowledge but also the reinterpretation and integration of existing knowledge. Firms draw on their past experiences, both within the current collaborative relationship and from previous collaborations, to inform their decision-making and adapt their governance mechanisms.

Furthermore, the organizational learning perspective recognizes that learning can occur at different levels within the organizations involved. Individual learning takes place as firms gain experience and develop expertise, which can then be shared and integrated into the collective knowledge at the level of the portfolio or the network of firms. The learning process is not limited to the individual level; it extends to relationship, portfolio, and the network as a whole, influencing the development of governance mechanisms at various levels.

While the experiential learning perspective highlights the incremental and local nature of the learning process, the interorganizational learning perspective acknowledges that this focus on the immediate context and problem-solving may limit firms' ability to be far-sighted in their governance development. However, by continuously engaging in learning processes and adapting their governance mechanisms, firms can build capabilities that enhance their ability to address future challenges and opportunities.

In summary, the learning perspective provides a broader framework for understanding the development of interorganizational governance mechanisms. It emphasizes the collective learning processes between firms and the importance of both explicit and tacit knowledge in shaping these mechanisms. By recognizing the dynamic and ongoing nature of learning, organizations can leverage their accumulated knowledge to improve their collaborative capabilities and develop governance arrangements that are responsive and effective.

3.2.3 Evolutionary Approach to Governance of IORs

The evolutionary perspective offers valuable insights into the development of interorganizational governance mechanisms by emphasizing the mutual and path-dependent influences between an organization and its environment. Building upon this angle, scholars have explored the dynamics of interorganizational relationships and the evolutionary processes that shape the governance mechanisms employed (Greve, 2017).

One notable study that contributes to our understanding of alliance evolution is Doz's (1996) examination of evolutionary processes in alliances. This research represents a significant contribution to process research in the alliance domain. While the study primarily focused on the evolutionary learning that occurs about the partner, rather than explicit knowledge transfer between the partners, it addresses a crucial managerial issue: what happens when firms form alliances with limited knowledge of their partners and how they operate?

The evolutionary perspective recognizes that interorganizational relationships are subject to continuous adaptation and change, driven by both internal and external dynamics. From an evolutionary standpoint, firms engage in a learning process as they interact and collaborate with their partners. This learning process involves the accumulation of knowledge, the development of new capabilities, and the emergence of novel governance mechanisms.

The concept of path dependence is integral to the evolutionary perspective. Path dependence refers to the idea that past events and decisions influence current actions and shape the future trajectory of organizations. In the context of interorganizational governance mechanisms, this means that early choices and experiences in the relationship can have long-lasting effects and determine the subsequent development of governance structures.

The evolutionary perspective acknowledges that when firms form alliances or engage in interorganizational collaborations, there may be limited knowledge about their partners and how they operate. In such cases, the learning process is a key driver of the evolution of governance mechanisms. Firms learn about their partners' capabilities, preferences, and ways of working as they engage in joint activities and navigate the collaborative relationship.

Through this evolutionary learning process, firms gain insights into their partners' strengths, weaknesses, and organizational cultures. They adapt their governance mechanisms to align with the emerging knowledge and understanding of their partners. The initial lack of knowledge about the partner may lead to a gradual exploration and exploitation of the collaboration's potential, shaping the development of governance mechanisms over time.

The evolutionary perspective also recognizes that the development of interorganizational governance mechanisms is influenced by external environmental factors. Firms adapt to the changing dynamics of their environment, including market conditions, industry trends, and technological advancements. The governance mechanisms employed reflect the firms' responses to these external forces and their efforts to navigate and survive within the evolving landscape.

Furthermore, the evolutionary perspective highlights that the development of interorganizational governance mechanisms is not a linear or predetermined process. It is subject to variation, selection, and retention dynamics, akin to the principles of biological evolution. Different governance mechanisms are tested and selected based on their effectiveness in achieving desired outcomes and addressing challenges. Successful mechanisms are retained and further refined, while less effective ones may be abandoned or modified (Nelson & Winter, 1982).

In summary, the evolutionary perspective provides a valuable lens for understanding the development of interorganizational governance mechanisms. It highlights the mutual and path-dependent influences between interorganizational relationships and their environments. By considering the evolutionary dynamics of interorganizational relationships, organizations can adapt their governance mechanisms to align with the emerging knowledge of their partners and respond to changing external factors. This perspective enhances our understanding of how governance mechanisms evolve over time and contributes to the design and management of effective interorganizational collaborations.

3.2.4 *Political Approach to Governance of IORs*

The political perspective provides a valuable lens through which we can understand the development of interorganizational governance mechanisms. Scholars, such as Brattström and Faems (2020), have articulated this perspective, shedding light on how IORS can serve as a battleground for political action and influence internal fragmentation within organizations.

One key aspect of the political perspective is the recognition that different coalitions within organizations may utilize IORS as a means of advancing their own interests and agendas. IORS can become arenas for political manoeuvring, where various factions within organizations compete for power, resources, and influence. These coalitions may seek to shape the governance mechanisms employed in the relationship to align with their own goals and priorities.

The political perspective emphasizes that IORs can have profound effects on internal fragmentation within organizations. As different coalitions vie for control and influence over the relationship, conflicts and power struggles may arise. These struggles can lead to internal divisions and fragmentation within the organization, as different groups seek to assert their interests and agendas.

In understanding interorganizational relational dynamics, the political perspective offers insights that complement existing research. It highlights that when one of the partner organizations is highly fragmented, the mechanisms typically theorized in extant research to explain relational dynamics, such as reinforcing spirals, are less likely to emerge. Instead, the political perspective points to a set of politically charged mechanisms that can fuel the emergence of dual relational dynamics as an alternative pattern.

Dual relational dynamics refer to situations where the IOR simultaneously exhibits cooperative and conflictual behaviors. This pattern can arise when the different coalitions within organizations engage in strategic actions to promote their own interests and undermine rival factions. The political perspective brings attention to the power struggles, negotiations, and conflicts that shape these dual dynamics and influence the evolution of interorganizational governance mechanisms.

Within the political perspective, interorganizational relationships are viewed as inherently political arenas, where power dynamics and struggles for influence play a central role. These power dynamics can influence the development and design of governance mechanisms, as different coalitions seek to shape the rules, decision-making processes, and resource allocations within the relationship.

Furthermore, the political perspective highlights the importance of understanding the broader institutional and environmental context within which IORs operate. Institutional pressures and political factors outside the immediate dyadic relationship can shape the power dynamics and influence the development of governance mechanisms. Political considerations, such as regulations, industry norms, and stakeholder pressures, can shape the constraints and opportunities for organizations engaged in interorganizational relationships IORs.

In summary, the political perspective offers a valuable understanding of the development of interorganizational governance mechanisms. It recognizes that IORs can be sites of political action and influence internal fragmentation within organizations. By exploring the power struggles, conflicts, and negotiations that occur within and between organizations, this perspective enriches our understanding of interorganizational relational dynamics. It highlights the political nature of governance mechanisms and emphasizes the importance of considering broader institutional and environmental factors. Incorporating the political perspective enhances our ability to comprehend and manoeuvre the complex dynamics of IORs.

3.3 Governance Mechanism's Replication

To effectively manage IORs for innovation, firms must develop a clear governance strategy for their external relationships to leverage learning opportunities and enhance their innovation performance. This involves maneuvering through the complexities of balancing exploration and exploitation, as discussed by the knowledge-based approach (Winter et al., 2012) and the resource-based view of the firm firm (Barney, 1991; Penrose, 1959). Firms face the "replication dilemma," where they must choose between innovating through the experimentation of new solutions or leveraging their existing capabilities through replication (Winter & Szulanski, 2001, p. 737). The trade-off usually represented by this axis is that between the advantages of finding new ad-hoc solutions (learning and adaptation) and those of replicating firm's consolidated routines (precision and efficiency) (D'Adderio, 2014).

The perspectives of problem-solving, organizational learning, evolutionary, and political provide distinct explanations for the need to replicate governance forms across different interorganizational relationships. In the upcoming subsections, we first establish a framework that defines replication strategies, and then we explore the reasons behind firms' decisions to replicate or not replicate these governance approaches.

3.3.1 Defining Replication Strategies

Within the realm of IORs governance, firms can draw on their previous experiences in managing external partners, which contribute to the development of their relational capabilities in the form of inter-firm relational routines, promoting stability. Conversely, firms may also seek novel and ad-hoc governance solutions to address specific IORs or a set of IORs, adapting their governance approach to unique circumstances. The management challenge associated with collaborative innovation, which is inherently complex and ambiguous, intensifies the tension between pursuing stability through replication and embracing change through ad-hoc solutions. Change, on one hand, has the potential to enhance the effectiveness of organizational processes, enabling innovation and the adoption of tailored solutions (D'Adderio, 2014). As firms engage in the development of organizational practices, including the management of IORs, they accumulate new experiences, enhancing their internal knowledge base (Zollo et al., 2002). In the context of IORs, a customized approach can elicit a more positive response from the counterpart, fostering trust and reducing concerns about potential exploitation by the firm (Szulanski & Jensen, 2008). However, in resource-constrained contexts such as innovation, the ability to effectively leverage knowledge becomes a crucial source of competitive advantage (Winter & Szulanski, 2001). Replication serves as the process by which firms address the challenge of knowledge utilization (Winter & Szulanski, 2001), enabling the transfer of learning from one context to another. For instance, successful governance approaches, whether formal, informal, or a combination of both, previously employed in collaborative projects, are replicated and applied to other IORs. Moreover, in replicating successful practices, firms recreate the complex knowledge system underpinning those solutions (Szulanski & Jensen, 2008), facilitating absorption and knowledge diffusion within the organization (Zollo & Winter, 2002). The strategy of replicating organizational practices signifies the firm's accumulated capability (Szulanski, 1996; Winter, 1995), reflecting the completion of the knowledge transfer process through which the organization establishes and sustains a set of routines in new settings. Over time, the organization refines its ability to manage this process through experience and repetition (Winter & Szulanski, 2001). Thus, the replication process in IORs governance serves as a catalyst for building relational capabilities within the organization.

3.3.2 Unravelling the Replication of Governance Forms Through a Multi-perspective Analysis

Each of the four outlined perspectives on the evolution of governance mechanisms in IORs presents a distinct lens that allows us to comprehend the underlying rationales and mechanisms that facilitate the replication of governance structures. By examining each of these perspectives individually, we gain the ability to uncover and analyse the replication processes from a multi-dimensional lens. The problem-solving perspective suggests that the complexity of a problem influences the optimal method of solution search and the means of organizing that search (Nickerson & Zenger, 2004). Different governance alternatives are matched in a discriminating way to problems based on their associated benefits and costs in governing solution search (Hoetker & Mellewigt, 2009). In this context, replicating governance forms across IORs can be seen as a way to address similar problem complexities consistently. From this perspective, paraphrasing Kogut and Zander (1996) firms "know more than what their contracts can say", therefore replication is a necessity because knowledge is ambiguous (Williams, 2007) and the firm is not able to separate what depends on the different contexts. By replicating effective governance forms, organizations can ensure that the same tried and tested approaches are applied to similar problems, optimizing the likelihood, speed, and cost-effectiveness of finding valuable solutions.

Similarly, the experiential learning perspective emphasizes the importance of knowledge acquisition and adaptation. Firms engage in a continuous learning process through their interactions with partners in interorganizational relationships. Replicating governance forms across relationships allows organizations to transfer and leverage the knowledge and insights gained from previous collaborations (Mayer & Argyres, 2004). Therefore, replication is useful because of the knowledge differential presents in the different relationships. In a relationship a typical argument of replication is that replicating successful governance forms, organizations can build on their prior learning and apply proven approaches to similar situations, reducing uncertainty and increasing the likelihood of positive outcomes (Park & Puranam, 2020).

The evolutionary perspective recognizes the role of path dependence and learning in shaping interorganizational relationships. Replicating governance forms can be viewed as a result of organizations' evolutionary processes, whereby past choices and experiences influence current actions. Path-dependent influences may lead organizations to replicate governance forms that have been successful in the past, as these forms are seen as familiar, reliable, and aligned with the organization's capabilities. Replication allows organizations to build on their established competencies and adapt them to new contexts, promoting stability and efficiency (Nelson & Winter, 1982). But further developing this argument, replication is also useful for firms to avoid remaining stuck in suboptimal governance solution. Indeed, replication can help to deviate from how they would have acted if restricted to their own experience obtained from learning-by-doing (move out of secondary paths) (Park & Puranam, 2021, 2023).

Finally, the value replication may derive from the mechanism of isomorphism and legitimization (DiMaggio & Powell, 1983). This perspective emphasizes the power struggles and political dynamics within interorganizational relationships. Replicating governance forms can be driven by the need to establish and maintain power, control, and influence over the relationship. Different coalitions within organizations may seek to replicate governance forms that align with their interests and agendas. Replication can serve as a strategic move to ensure that the governance mechanisms favour a particular coalition or protect their influence within the relationship. By replicating governance forms, organizations can assert their power and maintain a sense of control over the relationship.

However, while these angles suggest the value of replicating over time and across relationships of familiar governance approaches (Brattström & Faems, 2020; Mayer & Argyres, 2004; Winter & Szulanski, 2001), firms must also recognize the contingent and dynamic nature of governance in interorganizational relationships. Various factors, such as the nature of the innovation, stage of the process, attributes of the partner, shifts in the external environment, power dynamics, interdependence, organizational inertia, loss of partner-specific learning, and unquestioned assumptions should prompt nuanced evaluation of replication's merits versus needs for tailored governance (Hoetker & Mellewigt, 2009; Nickerson & Zenger, 2004).

Indeed, a nuanced understanding of the contextual landscape can unlock numerous possibilities for implementing more tailored governance mechanisms (Williams, 2007). The management of these contextual contingencies is particularly crucial, especially in scenarios involving disruptive innovations that demand heightened flexibility. Conversely, in less adaptable environments, such as those characteristics of incremental innovations, the preference may lean towards the continued use of customized governance mechanisms. Replicating established governance structures in contexts demanding flexibility poses the risk of inertia, hindering the exploration of innovative partnership opportunities. This underscores the importance of adopting a balanced and contextually aware approach, strategically employing tailored governance in response to specific situational demands. Such an approach ensures adaptability to dynamic contingencies, fostering the exploration of diverse collaboration avenues.

Moreover, the configuration of governance may necessitate tailoring to a partner's specific size, cultural dynamics, past collaboration experiences, and other unique attributes, which might assume varying significance across distinct phases of the inter-organizational collaboration. In the initial stages, firms may intensify adaptive measures. However, as IORs accumulate experience, they exhibit a resistance to change, and demand more structured governance.

The study underscores the significance of replication as a crucial mechanism for the governance of IORs shedding light on how the adaptability of replication is shaped by contextual factors within the knowledge environment, determining the level of ambiguity linked to targeted knowledge. While achieving replication in disrupted settings may prove challenging, and outright successful copying might be elusive, our study underscores that investing effort in the replication process substantially enhances the transfer of valuable knowledge.

However, overemphasizing replication risks blind spots regarding the diverse forms it takes in practice and its variable effectiveness for creating competitive advantages. While the replication of existing governance mechanisms might be an effective reaction in the face of the uncertainty that typically characterizes innovation projects (Haunschild & Miner, 1997), it may also hamper firms' readiness to change when they have to coordinate with partners, increasing the unintended problems stemming from such adaptation (Winter & Szulanski, 2001). Firms face trade-offs in routinizing governance mechanisms. Practices successful in one IOR may not seamlessly transfer to another, raising dilemmas over replicating existing approaches or innovating to meet new demands.

The tension between replicating existing governance practices and innovating new approaches manifests at multiple levels during the transfer of governance mechanisms across interorganizational relationships. At a broad level, firms may manage this trade-off by establishing an orderly sequence that prioritizes exploration and innovation in early stages of a partnership, followed by exploitation and replication as the collaboration matures. However, conflicting pressures for innovation versus replication might emerge at the micro level, as the individuals and teams involved in governance transfer continually grapple with balancing replication and innovation throughout the collaboration process. Replication provides familiarity and stability, while innovation addresses emerging contingencies. Particular collaboration phases may benefit from emphasizing one over the other and individuals must regularly re-evaluate and re-negotiate the balance between leveraging existing governance knowledge versus creating tailored new practices responsive to specific contextual needs. This fluid tension management occurs iteratively at the ground level as collaborations progress, rather than through monolithic firm-level sequences. The innovation-replication balance manifests as an ongoing dilemma for practitioners managing the transfer of governance mechanisms across fluid and evolving interorganizational relationships (D'Adderio, 2014).

The specific context of the interorganizational relationship is crucial in determining how these micro-level tensions between innovation and replication are managed by individuals and teams. Characteristics like the degree of novelty in the collaboration, prior shared experience between partners, and phase of the innovation process all influence whether emphasizing replication of existing governance practices or innovating new customized approaches is most suitable. Rather than wholly separate governance practices, individuals may dynamically and selectively emphasize one tension over the other at specific points based on contextual demands. Firms can develop a repertoire of governance mechanisms that are fine-tuned through slight variations that result to be both innovative and replication of previous governance templates. The resulting governance mechanisms are not static or universally applied—they adaptively evolve as individuals configure and reconfigure them to respond to the particular contexts posed by combinations of partners, teams, and networks that shape the goals of each interorganizational relationship.

In conclusion, this examination of replication reveals nuances beyond its simple advantages. While replication provides stability amidst uncertainty, overemphasis risks inflexibility and inability to meet context-specific needs. Effective governance likely entails maintaining balanced tensions between innovation and replication and highlighting replication's contingent and evolving nature rather than its routinized application. Individuals and firms who develop dynamic governance repertoires tailored to partnership contexts gain advantages. Further research can enrich theoretical perspectives on how to best achieve this balance and optimize the strategic use of replication while avoiding its blind spots and limitations. Insights into the multi-level tensions, context-dependent applications, and interplay with innovation advance more nuanced understanding of replication's complex role in IORs governance.

3.4 Conclusion

The study of the governance mechanisms for IORs raises issues such as the decision of the effective means to control the complexity of the exchanges, but also the capabilities required to develop and adjust the governance mechanisms. The account of the theoretical perspective that we offer highlights the importance of the adjustment process as an important source of variation in firm performance and growth as they represent the procedures by which social relationships are created and coordinated in the IOR context.

In conclusion, this chapter has examined the importance of understanding the evolution and approaches of governance in IORs. By exploring four perspectives—problem-solving, learning, evolutionary, and political—we have highlighted the value of replicating governance mechanisms across relationships to address similar problem complexities, leverage knowledge and insights, adapt established competencies to new contexts, and assert power and control. However, while replication offers benefits, the contingent value and effectiveness of different governance modes across relationships should be considered to avoid limiting adaptability and hindering firms' readiness for change in innovation projects.

Understanding the processes that drive the replication and adjustment of governance mechanisms in IORs is crucial for several reasons. IORs are complex and dynamic arrangements involving multiple organizations working towards common goals. Governance mechanisms coordinate activities, manage relationships, and align interests among participants. By comprehending the evolution and mechanisms of governance, researchers and practitioners gain insights into how relationships develop, evolve, and function over time.

Governance mechanisms also shape organizational behavior and decision-making within IORs, influencing resource allocation, risk-sharing, information sharing, and decision authority. Understanding these mechanisms enables organizations to design and implement governance structures suitable for their objectives, effectively managing challenges and uncertainties in interorganizational collaborations.

The evolution of governance mechanisms highlights the need for adaptation and learning as relationships encounter new challenges. By studying this evolution, best practices, lessons learned, and strategies for improving governance design and implementation in IORs can be identified.

Furthermore, governance mechanisms play a vital role in value creation and appropriation within IORs, facilitating cooperation, innovation, knowledge sharing, and resource utilization. Understanding what drives value creation enables organizations to optimize their governance strategies and enhance their competitive advantage.

Finally, studying the evolution of and approaches to governance in IORs contributes to theory development and expands knowledge in management and organizational studies. It helps refine existing theories, develop new frameworks, and generate insights that advance our understanding of interorganizational dynamics, collaboration, and strategic management.

In summary, grasping governance evolution and approaches is vital for effective collaboration, value creation, and adaptation. It enables organizations to design and implement governance structures aligned with their goals, successfully manage the intricacies of joint initiatives in IORS, and informs managerial practices in collaborative endeavours.

References

Barney, J. (1991). Firm resources and sustained competitive advantage. *Journal of Management, 17*(1), 99–120.

Brattström, A., & Faems, D. (2020). Interorganizational relationships as political battlefields: How fragmentation within organizations shapes relational dynamics between organizations. *Academy of Management Journal, 63*(5), 1591–1620. https://doi.org/10.5465/amj.2018.0038

Cyert, R. M., & March, J. G. (1963). *A behavioral theory of the firm* (Vol. 66). Prentice Hall.

D'Adderio, L. (2014). The replication dilemma unravelled: How organizations enact multiple goals in routine transfer. *Organization Science, 25*(5), 1325–1350.

Das, T. K., & Teng, B.-S. (1998). Between trust and control: Developing confidence in partner cooperation in alliances. *Academy of Management Review, 23*(3), 491–512.

DiMaggio, P. J., & Powell, W. W. (1983). The iron cage revisited: Institutional isomorphism and collective rationality in organizational fields. *American Sociological Review, 48*(2), 147–160. http://www.jstor.org/stable/2095101

Doz, Y. L. (1996). The evolution of cooperation in strategic alliances: Initial conditions or learning processes? *Strategic Management Journal, 17*(S1), 55–83.

Faems, D., Janssens, M., Madhok, A., & Looy, B. V. (2008). Toward an integrative perspective on alliance governance: Connecting contract design, trust dynamics, and contract application. *Academy of Management Journal, 51*(6), 1053–1078. https://doi.org/10.5465/amj.2008.35732527

Foss, N. J., & Weber, L. (2016). Moving opportunism to the back seat: Bounded rationality, costly conflict, and hierarchical forms. *The Academy of Management Review, 41*(1), 61–79. https://www.jstor.org/stable/43699319

Greve, H. R. (2017). Interorganizational evolution. In J. A. C. Baum (Ed.), *The Blackwell companion to organizations* (pp. 557–578). Blackwell Publishing Ltd.

Haunschild, P. R., & Miner, A. S. (1997). Modes of interorganizational imitation: The effects of outcome salience and uncertainty. *Administrative Science Quarterly, 42*(3), 472–500.

Hoetker, G., & Mellewigt, T. (2009). Choice and performance of governance mechanisms: Matching alliance governance to asset type. *Strategic Management Journal, 30*(10), 1025–1044. https://doi.org/10.1002/smj.775

Keller, A., Lumineau, F., Mellewigt, T., & Ariño, A. (2021). Alliance governance mechanisms in the face of disruption. *Organization Science, 32*(6), 1542–1570. https://doi.org/10.1287/orsc.2021.1437

Kogut, B., & Zander, U. (1992). Knowledge of the firm, combinative capabilities, and the replication of technology. *Organization Science, 3*(3), 383–397. https://doi.org/10.1287/orsc.3.3.383

Kogut, B., & Zander, U. (1996). What firms do? Coordination, identity, and learning. *Organization Science, 7*(5), 502–518. http://www.jstor.org/stable/2635287

Mayer, K. J., & Argyres, N. S. (2004). Learning to contract: Evidence from the personal computer industry. *Organization Science, 15*(4), 394–410.

Nelson, R. R., & Winter, S. G. (1982). The schumpeterian tradeoff revisited. *The American Economic Review, 72*(1), 114–132.

Nickerson, J. A., & Zenger, T. R. (2004). A knowledge-based theory of the firm—The problem-solving perspective. *Organization Science, 15*(6), 617–632.

Park, S., & Puranam, P. (2020). *Learning what they think vs. learning what they do: The micro-foundations of vicarious learning.* arXiv preprint arXiv:2007.15264

Park, S., & Puranam, P. (2021). Self-confirming biased beliefs in organizational "learning by doing." *Complexity, 2021,* 1–14. https://doi.org/10.1155/2021/8865872

Park, S., & Puranam, P. (2023). Vicarious learning without knowledge differentials. *Management Science.* https://doi.org/10.1287/mnsc.2023.4842

Penrose, E. (1959). *The theory of the growth of the firm.* Wiley.

Poppo, L., & Zhou, K. Z. (2014). Managing contracts for fairness in buyer–supplier exchanges. *Strategic Management Journal, 35*(10), 1508–1527. https://doi.org/10.1002/smj.2175

Reuer, J. J., & Ariño, A. (2007). Strategic alliance contracts: Dimensions and determinants of contractual complexity. *Strategic Management Journal, 28*(3), 313–330. https://doi.org/10.1002/smj.581

Schepker, D. J., Oh, W.-Y., Martynov, A., & Poppo, L. (2014). The many futures of contracts: Moving beyond structure and safeguarding to coordination and adaptation. *Journal of Management, 40*(1), 193–225. https://doi.org/10.1177/0149206313491289

Schilke, O., & Cook, K. S. (2013). A cross-level process theory of trust development in interorganizational relationships. *Strategic Organization, 11*(3), 281–303. https://doi.org/10.1177/1476127012472096

Szulanski, G. (1996). Exploring internal stickiness: Impediments to the transfer of best practice within the firm. *Strategic Management Journal, 17*(S2), 27–43. https://doi.org/10.1002/smj.4250171105

Szulanski, G., & Jensen, R. J. (2008). Growing through copying: The negative consequences of innovation on franchise network growth. *Research Policy, 37*(10), 1732–1741. https://doi.org/10.1016/j.respol.2008.08.012

Weick, K. E. (1976). Educational organizations as loosely coupled systems. *Administrative Science Quarterly, 21*(1), 1–19. https://doi.org/10.2307/2391875

Williams, S. (2007). A supplier development programme: The SME experience. *Journal of Small Business and Enterprise Development.*

Winter, S. G. (1995). Four Rs of profitability: Rents, resources, routines, and replication. In *Resource-based and evolutionary theories of the firm: Towards a synthesis* (pp. 147–178). Springer.

Winter, S. G., & Szulanski, G. (2001). Replication as strategy. *Organization Science, 12*(6), 730–743. https://doi.org/10.1287/orsc.12.6.730.10084

Winter, S. G., Szulanski, G., Ringov, D., & Jensen, R. J. (2012). Reproducing knowledge: Inaccurate replication and failure in franchise organizations. *Organization Science, 23*(3), 672–685.

Zaheer, A., McEvily, B., & Perrone, V. (1998). Does trust matter? Exploring the effects of interorganizational and interpersonal trust on performance. *Organization Science, 9*(2), 141–159. http://www.jstor.org/stable/2640350

Zollo, M., & Winter, S. G. (2002). Deliberate learning and the evolution of dynamic capabilities. *Organization Science, 13*(3), 339–351.

Zollo, M., Reuer, J. J., & Singh, H. (2002). Interorganizational routines and performance in strategic alliances. *Organization Science, 13*(6), 701–713. https://doi.org/10.1287/orsc.13.6.701.503

CHAPTER 4

Collaborative Innovation in the Italian Automotive Supply-Chain

Abstract This chapter investigates the interorganizational relationships and dynamics of innovation within the automotive industry, characterized by a hierarchical structure involving original equipment manufacturers (OEMs) and specialized suppliers. This structure fosters extensive information sharing and close collaboration among the actors. The results emphasize the importance of making effective governance choices and developing strong relationships for Italian automotive suppliers in order to navigate technological transitions successfully and achieve collaborative innovation performance. The study reveals that governance choices, which are influenced by contextual factors and organizational practices, can either facilitate or impede innovation outcomes. While informal mechanisms have traditionally played a vital role in collaborative innovation, their effectiveness may be diminished in contexts of high technological uncertainty and intense industry competition. The findings underscore the critical need to comprehend governance choices and interorganizational relationships for suppliers operating in the innovation-driven automotive industry, particularly during periods of significant change.

Keywords Governance choices · Automotive industry · Technological transitions · Buyer-Suppliers' relationships · Collaborative innovation

© The Author(s), under exclusive license to Springer Nature Switzerland AG 2024
S. Li Pira and A. Moretti, *Governing Interorganizational Relationships for Innovation*,
https://doi.org/10.1007/978-3-031-50229-3_4

4.1 Innovation in the Automotive Industry

The automotive industry is a central sector for the European economy, both in terms of its contribution to economic value generation (estimated at approximately 4% of European GDP) and its direct or indirect employment of over 12 million people. The industry's significance to the European and national economies makes competitiveness and sustainability key priorities for policymakers. In an environment characterized by increasing competitive pressure and a reconfiguration of the competitive landscape, it is recognized that the competitiveness of the automotive supply chain is driven by technological innovation dynamics in both product and process dimensions. The automotive industry operates on a tiered supply system, with original equipment manufacturers (OEMs) acting as leaders in vertical supply chains. The supply chain consists of a small number of large suppliers at higher tiers and numerous specialized small and medium-sized firms at lower tiers. Innovation and product development tasks are distributed throughout the supply chain via close relationships, which are crucial for driving innovation performance in firms (Clark & Fujimoto, 1991; Helper & Sako, 1995, 2010; Sako, 2004). Due to the complex product architecture and strong interdependence among components and systems, OEMs and suppliers are compelled to engage in extensive information sharing during all stages of product development (Jean et al., 2014). While OEMs retain expertise in system integration and control, suppliers predominantly design and manufacture components and systems, following a hierarchical supply chain structure (Takeishi, 2001, 2002).

However, these innovative processes must be understood in light of the profound changes that have occurred in the roles and dynamics between OEMs and suppliers over the past thirty years (Moretti & Zirpoli, 2017a). By the end of the 1980s, carmakers' push towards production outsourcing stemmed from the growing industry-wide belief that outsourcing a significant portion of production had become a competitive necessity (Whitford, 2005, p. 57). The rise of the Japanese low vertical integration model increased the influence of suppliers (Schulze et al., 2015), and car manufacturers were encouraged to focus on design, assembly, and marketing. On the other hand, suppliers suddenly found themselves invested with entirely new responsibilities, leading them to reorganize into what is referred to as the vertical supply network (Zirpoli, 2010). This network was characterized by a hierarchical stratification of highly specialized firms, directly linked only to first-tier suppliers (and thus no longer in direct contact with the final assemblers). In these years, the dominant approach was to segment and classify suppliers based on the complexity and strategic relevance of the exchanged product (Schulze et al., 2015). Direct suppliers had to make significant investments to integrate themselves with the assembler's processes, providing complete or partially assembled modules, and actively participating in the design and development processes (Whitford, 2005). The efforts and investments required to remain a direct supplier (in terms of capabilities, capacity, and infrastructure) led to a self-selection process among the OEM's supply base, with some companies leaving the industry while others positioned themselves at the base of the pyramid, becoming second or third-tier suppliers (providing components to first-tier suppliers) (Zirpoli, 2010). These particular conditions, resulting from the industry's reconfiguration, necessitated not only mutual adaptation processes between carmakers and suppliers but also significant coordination activities and processes with other actors in the production network. This was done to ensure maximum consistency among all processes and product components in an environment characterized by distributed innovation processes (Moretti & Zirpoli, 2017a).

This production process configuration gave rise to an intense network of interdependencies among all actors involved at various levels in outsourcing practices. Nonetheless, carmakers maintained full control over the final assembly process, as automotive production requires both system integration capabilities and economies of scale (Jacobides et al., 2016).

The transition from large inventories to just-in-time production in the early 2000s compelled OEMs to rely more heavily on supplier assistance for process and product innovation, enabling rapid transformation of new ideas into marketable products. This necessitated strong cooperation and information transfer between firms (Jean et al., 2014; Whitford & Zeitlin, 2004). OEMs fostered "closer relationships with a core 'strategic' group, sharing ideas, technology, and costs in ways that may benefit competitors but also foster learning among smaller firms, ultimately transforming the supply base into a valuable source of new ideas and technology" (Whitford & Zeitlin, 2004, p. 13).

This organizational complexity still resembles the current automotive production system, characterized by a vertical network with the OEM at the top and a hierarchical stratification of suppliers at lower levels based on the strategic relevance of the exchanged product. Such complexity is further stressed by the centrality of innovation processes for manufacturers' competitiveness, especially in these times of transition. Manufacturers must manage co-engineering practices, distributed competencies, and knowledge (Lee & Berente, 2012). In such an empirical context, inter-organizational relationships for innovative processes become a topic of crucial relevance (Gulati et al., 2000).

The strong focus of past literature on the OEMs' perspective allowed to explore in-depth their role in the automotive innovation network, emphasizing their strategies in managing their vertical networks (Takeishi, 2001, 2002; Zirpoli & Becker, 2011a, 2011b). These studies have highlighted how the innovative capacity of the supply chain is often driven by OEMs, who are interested in reorganizing their outsourcing relationships by reducing the number of suppliers and fostering specialization while establishing a dense collaboration network with second and third-tier suppliers (Whitford & Zeitlin, 2004). The reorganization of the vertical supply pyramid based on pragmatic collaboration (Helper et al., 2000) has facilitated the development of innovation-oriented relationships and knowledge sharing among supplier firms through learning-by-monitoring processes, where firms advance their own knowledge through collaboration with partners while controlling potential opportunistic behaviors in the exchange (Sabel, 1996).

However, the focus on the role of OEMs, has resulted in limited empirical knowledge about the evolution of the automotive supply chain context, particularly regarding the effects of consolidated distributed innovation models on the innovation performance of suppliers.

4.2 Innovating in the Italian Automotive Industry

The pivotal role of OEMs in driving innovation within their entire supply network is particularly relevant in empirical contexts like Italy, where the automotive industry has been predominantly dominated by a single player—Fiat Auto, later Fiat Chrysler Automobiles (FCA), and currently

Stellantis.[1] The Italian automotive industry is primarily characterized by a sole OEM and a supply chain comprising numerous small and medium-sized suppliers that have historically relied on Fiat-FCA (Moretti & Zirpoli, 2017b). Consequently, the presence of a dominant manufacturer has fostered a highly interconnected vertical chain, wherein all industry-related small and medium-sized enterprises (SMEs) collaborate and share knowledge and competencies to promote collective product and process innovation activities (Calabrese, 2020; Calabrese & Erbetta, 2004; Moretti, 2018; Moretti & Zirpoli, 2017b, 2021; Zirpoli & Caputo, 2002).

During the past two decades, a series of events unfolded, leading to a profound crisis in the Italian automotive industry. Firstly, the internationalization process of FCA shifted the balance between activities in Italy and the US, resulting in increasing peripheralization of the Italian side. Subsequently, the economic crisis struck, triggering an international automotive market crisis and an upsurge in competition from Asian rivals. More recently, the pandemic, along with semiconductor shortages and the acquisition of FCA by the Stellantis group, exacerbated the critical situation of the Italian industry as a peripheral market and production site within a shrinking European market. Consequently, there has been a significant decline in vehicle production in Italy, leading to a corresponding decrease in the domestic market for suppliers (Calabrese, 2020). The overall production of cars and commercial vehicles in Italy declined from approximately 2 million in 1990 to 1.7 million in 2000, slightly over 800,000 in 2010, and around 750,000 in 2020. In Europe, the total production of motor vehicles in 2021 reached 16.331 million, with historically competitive countries like Germany (3.309 million), Spain (2.098 million), and France (1.351 million) surpassing Italian production levels. Additionally, the Czech Republic (1.111 million), Slovakia (1 million), and the United Kingdom (932,000) exceeded Italian production levels. Consequently, among European producing countries, Italy only ranks ahead of Poland (439,000 vehicles) in terms of production levels in 2021 (Moretti & Zirpoli, 2023).

---

[1] In 2021 the year commenced with the establishment of the Stellantis group, resulting from the equal merger of Fiat Chrysler and PSA, officially completed on January 16, 2021. The merger was undertaken by the two manufacturers to address the demands of the evolving automotive industry, including the challenge of electrification.

Against this backdrop, as the green transition gained momentum and the industry experienced a turbulent era of technological change, the boundaries of the automotive sector were being reshaped, creating opportunities for new entrants and placing significant pressures on incumbents to adapt and navigate through the transformation. In response to these challenges, Italian suppliers, confronted with intense global competition and mounting competitive pressures, recognized the importance of leveraging their IORs as a valuable source of innovation to enhance their competitiveness in the global automotive industry (Whitford & Enrietti, 2005).

4.3 The EVs Transition of the Automotive Industry

When industries face turbulent times due to a shifting technological paradigm, innovation becomes necessary for the survival of firms (Anderson & Tushman, 1990). Therefore, it is particularly suitable to study how to effectively govern innovation in the automotive industry. The automotive industry is currently undergoing one of the most significant changes it has experienced in the last century. After decades of stability, the technological paradigm has now shifted towards a new concept of the product. Automobiles now require new, more sustainable powertrains, which have significant implications for the overall structure of the product. The value of automobiles is now created through the services attached to them, and connectivity and information technology (IT) have become key dimensions for customer satisfaction and perception of product quality. These combined trends are having profound consequences for the global architecture of the automotive industry. The industry is transforming from a system of vertical networks, with the OEM or carmaker leading innovation processes and guiding the supply chain, to a new ecosystem (Jacobides et al., 2016). Platforms are now at the core of value creation processes, and many new players in the industry are assuming key roles in innovation and value creation.

In the European context, the European legislature's decision to phase out the production of internal combustion engine vehicles from 2035 onwards aligns with the general situation of the European automotive industry, characterized by two trends: one long-term and one contingent. The first trend manifests as a decline in the demand for automobiles in Europe, driven by the reduced use of private mobility in urban centers, commonly known as the "peak-car" phenomenon (Bastian & Börjesson, 2015; Metz, 2013; Wittwer et al., 2019). This decline corresponds to changing preferences for car usage, especially among the younger generation, who are inclined to replace car ownership with long-term and short-term leasing. The second trend relates to European automobile production, which has experienced a significant decline since 2020 due to the COVID-19 crisis and the unavailability of components such as microchips or wiring. Hence, the phase-out set for 2035 is regarded as one of the most significant threats to the European automotive market. Incumbent players in the industry have been compelled to rapidly accelerate their innovation strategies towards sustainability and the development of green powertrains. This aggressive shift in focus is driven by the urgency to align with the changing regulatory landscape and meet the growing demand for environmentally friendly solutions. The phase-out deadline has created a sense of urgency for established companies to adapt and transform their product offerings, production processes, and overall business models to ensure long-term viability in the evolving market.

When it comes to the Italian automotive industry, these topics become even more relevant, as the technological transition has been considered particularly challenging in its specific innovation context (Moretti & Zirpoli, 2021a). Although exports and market diversification have significantly increased in recent years (with export value growing by +9.9% in 2021, surpassing Germany's +7% and France's +3%), Stellantis still accounts for an average of 50% of the turnover of the Italian automotive component sector. The heavy dependence of numerous firms in the supply chain on the procurement choices of the Italian carmaker has led Italian suppliers to adopt a passive approach to innovation. These firms simply wait for their sole customer to choose the technological direction, and then follow suit (Zirpoli, 2010). The general lack of a proactive approach to innovation remains one of the major weaknesses of Italian suppliers, who suffer from their peripheral position with respect to the European automotive decision-making centers. Furthermore, the situation becomes even more complex when considering Stellantis' production choices. Italian research and development (R&D) investments, in fact, depend on Stellantis' orders. When these orders decline, as has happened in recent years, Italian suppliers reduce their overall investments in R&D. This phenomenon clearly impacts Italian subsidiaries of suppliers belonging to foreign groups as well. In general, there is a tendency in Italy to follow the choices of manufacturers rather than anticipate them with product/process innovations. This tendency is likely a legacy of the dominance of Fiat, FCA, and now Stellantis in Italy (Moretti & Zirpoli, 2023).

Nevertheless, in these turbulent times characterized by technological discontinuities and the reorganization of the industry architecture, innovation is the only way for firms to survive and remain competitive in the market. Effectively managing intra- and inter-organizational innovation processes could be the core competence of firms operating in the automotive ecosystem, allowing them to leverage internal and external sources of innovation.

As emphasized in the preceding chapters, effective governance of innovation is crucial to achieve favorable performance outcomes for all parties involved in distributed innovation processes. The relational characteristics of the Italian supply chain play a critical role in exploring governance choices and their impact on firms' innovation performance. Given the historical context of the Italian automotive sector, tightly intertwined with a dominant player in the industry, the vertical network of suppliers has become highly dense and interconnected. This relational embeddedness of Italian suppliers serves as a protective factor against potential risks and hazards in their interorganizational relationships along the vertical chain, as engaging in opportunistic behavior would result in detrimental reputational consequences within such a close-knit network. However, due to the economic circumstances of the past decade, suppliers, particularly those in lower-tier positions, have faced intense competition among themselves to ensure their survival. Consequently, contractual power has become concentrated in the hands of the dominant carmaker and its first-tier or large suppliers. In such a context, firms are compelled to pursue both formal mechanisms to safeguard their contractual agreements and the reassurance provided by social relationships and mutual trust among partners. These social aspects complement the formal mechanisms and contribute to sustaining collaborative efforts (Poppo & Zenger, 2002).

4.4 The Case of the Italian Automotive Supply-Chain: Governance Choices and Innovation

In this section, we further explore Italian suppliers' governance choices for pursuing collaborative innovation outcomes, relying on data derived from the 2017, 2018, and 2019 waves of the National Observatory Survey on Italian Automotive Suppliers. This survey encompasses comprehensive information on all Italian firms operating within the automotive sector. The directory data obtained from the survey were cross-referenced with the registry of firms, utilizing the Nomenclature of Economic Activities (NACE) Rev.2 (ATECO 2007) sectoral identifiers associated with automotive suppliers. Additionally, supplementary updates were incorporated directly from the national industrial association of automotive suppliers. These measures were implemented to ensure the most accurate approximation of the population of Italian firms involved in the automotive industry, accounting for annual firm openings and closures. Moreover, updated information from the new National Observatory on the Transformations of the Automotive Ecosystem are used to assess how surveyed firms are exposed to the risk of the green transition, and whether they have already started to develop innovative projects for electric vehicles. By utilizing these different data sources, we can examine how Italian automotive suppliers choose to govern their IORs for innovation and how governance mechanisms diffuse (see Chapter 3). Moreover, we investigate how these choices are influenced by contextual relational characteristics (see Chapter 2). Additionally, we analyze the connection between these choices and suppliers' performance, their capacity to adapt their competencies to navigate the transition to electric vehicles (EVs), and their vulnerability to the challenges posed by the green transition.

The respondents to the survey[2] were asked to identify their three most important IORs for collaborative innovation, naming their partners. They provided the partners identification and characteristics (buyer/supplier relationship), and all the information about the strength, length, and

---

[2] The survey was distributed to the whole set of firms in the database of the National Observatory of Italian Automotive Suppliers (Moretti & Zirpoli, 2021b). The directory data were cross-referenced with the Nomenclature of Economic Activities (NACE) Rev.2 (ATECO 2007) sectoral identifiers associated with automotive suppliers, and additional updates were incorporated through the national industrial association of automotive suppliers. This comprehensive approach aimed to provide an accurate representation of Italian firms in the automotive industry, accounting for annual openings and closures. When possible, we contacted the firm's managing director or designated contact person, typically someone who had participated in previous studies or expressed an interest in participating. The survey was administered using an online questionnaire created on the Qualtrics platform (www.qualtrics.com). We employed strategies outlined by Dillman (2000) to maximize response rates. In total, 848 firms were surveyed across three waves, with an initial response rate of 38.4%. The breakdown of responses is as follows: 403 responses (21.1% initial response rate) in 2017, 467 responses (21.3% initial response rate) in 2018, and 551 responses (25% initial response rate) in 2019.

governance of these IORs (indicating their use of formal and informal mechanisms on a 1–5 Likert scale). We then build the dataset at the dyad level, using the IOR as the unit of analysis, at the portfolio level using the three main relationships as the unit of analysis, and at the network level building the network of relationships between all the respondents named by other interviewed suppliers. In total, the network sample comprises over 2200 dyads.

In the following sections, we aim to examine the influence of various exchange hazards on the governance choices of Italian automotive suppliers, drawing upon the theoretical foundations discussed in Chapter 2. We begin by exploring how contextual factors at the dyad, portfolio, and network levels of analysis shape these exchange hazards. Additionally, we investigate how firms determine the governance of their IORs, with a specific focus on the replication mechanism discussed in Chapter 3. We analyze the diffusion of governance practices within portfolios and networks. Finally, we conclude by discussing the impact of governance choices on firms' ability to tackle uncertain industry transitions resulting from shifts in the technological paradigm.

4.5 Exchange Hazards and the Choice of Governance Mechanisms

As discussed in Chapter 2, the characteristics of partners and the features of relationships play a significant role in shaping the exchange hazards associated with uncertainty and transaction-specific investments in interorganizational relationships. These exchange hazards, which are typically examined from a transaction-cost economic perspective, serve as contextual factors that drive firms' decisions regarding governance mechanisms. However, in order to gain a comprehensive understanding of the factors influencing IORs and firms' governance choices, it is crucial to recognize the multi-layered networks in which these relationships are embedded. Therefore, the analysis needs to expand beyond the dyadic level and encompass the portfolio and network levels. In the following subsections, we delve into these three levels, shedding light on how different contextual factors intertwine to influence firms' governance choices.

4.5.1 The Dyadic Level of Analysis

Data on Italian automotive suppliers allow us to explore factors related to both partners' and relationships' characteristics, such as: company's position along the supply-chain, size, power, and their relational embeddedness.

Table 4.1 presents the average values of the use of Informal and Formal mechanisms in firms' IORs, compared between partners' different features and between different relationships' features. Overall, the first emerging result is that formal mechanisms are consistently more used than informal ones, with values closer to 4 (on a 1–5 scale) the former and values closer to 2 the latter.

However, our main interest is in understanding if formal and informal mechanisms use changes depending on partners' characteristics and relational features.

In terms of supply chain position, firms collaborating with their suppliers report a higher utilization of informal mechanisms compared

Table 4.1 Partners' and relationships' features and governance choices

		Informal mechanisms	Formal mechanisms
Partners' features			
Supply-chain position	Client	2.19	3.65
	Supplier	2.41	3.52
Size	Large	1.76	4.21
	Medium	2.07	3.74
	Small	2.42	3.42
	Micro	2.88	3.11
Power	Tier 1	2.13	3.81
	Tier 2	2.29	3.51
	Tier 3	2.51	3.31
	Tier 4 and below	2.46	3.39
Relationship's features			
Relational embeddedness	Long duration	2.29	3.62
	Short duration	2.25	3.59
	High strength	2.24	3.65
	Low strength	2.27	3.54

Note The use of Formal and Informal Mechanisms are measured with a refined 5-point Likert scale ranging from 1 denoting negligible utilization to a rating of 5 indicating extensive and robust implementation to those collaborating with their clients. Conversely, when formal mechanisms are employed, firms cooperating with their customers adopt a more formal approach than those working with their suppliers.

As discussed in Chapter 2, both size and power influence exchange hazards in similar ways. Smaller and less powerful companies may perceive formal agreements as threatening and feel more comfortable with informal mechanisms. To examine the impact of firm size on our sample, we categorized firms as micro (less than 10 employees), small (between 10 and 50 employees), medium (between 50 and 250 employees), and large (over 250 employees). As a proxy for power asymmetries, we assessed the firm's position within the vertical innovation network, with tier 1 representing firms closest to the carmaker that drive innovation and market dynamics throughout the entire supply chain, as discussed in previous sections.

In terms of size, a clear pattern emerges regarding the use of formal and informal governance mechanisms: larger firms demonstrate lower usage of informality and a higher reliance on formality. A similar trend is observed for the power variable: firms located closer to the apex of the automotive supply chain pyramid exhibit a reduced reliance on informal coordination mechanisms and a greater emphasis on formal arrangements. The pattern deviates slightly for tier 4 and lower-level suppliers, where the increasing/decreasing trend is reversed. This outcome can be attributed to the fact that tier 4 suppliers are typically involved in commodity production and operate outside the industry's innovation dynamics due to their broader diversification across different sectors. Consequently, they experience less pronounced power dynamics compared to suppliers at tiers 1, 2, and 3.

In examining the characteristics of relationships, we utilized data on the relational embeddedness of the dyads under analysis. Consistent with existing literature, we measured relational embeddedness using two variables: relationship length and strength. Both variables were constructed using a 5-point Likert scale, where respondents were asked to indicate the duration (length) and frequency of their interactions (strength) with their partners. To investigate the impact of these two dimensions of relational embeddedness on firms' governance choices, we categorized the variables as long/short and high/low, respectively, based on whether they exceeded or fell below their respective means.

When partners are involved in longer relationships, they tend to employ higher levels of formal and informal governance mechanisms with respect to those involved in shorter relationships. The increased utilization of informal mechanisms can be attributed to the accumulated experience, familiarity, and social ties between the partners, which reduce uncertainty and mitigate the risk of opportunistic behavior. However, the increased use of formal mechanisms appears to contradict the expected outcome suggested by the literature. As discussed in Chapter 2, longer relationships are typically associated with a lower reliance on formal mechanisms. Nevertheless, our findings reveal only a marginal difference in the use of formality between long and short relationships. This could be explained by the intense competition prevalent in the Italian automotive supply chain, which necessitates the recourse to formal arrangements.

Similarly, the results concerning relationship strength, the other dimension of relational embeddedness, are somewhat counterintuitive. A clear pattern emerges: stronger relationships exhibit a higher propensity for formality and a lower propensity for informality.[3] When considering these results collectively, we are inclined to interpret them as indicative of a situation known in the literature as over-embeddedness. This occurs when excessively close ties cease to be beneficial for partners and instead exhibit detrimental effects within the relational dynamics.

4.5.2 *The Portfolio Level of Analysis*

As discussed in Chapter 2, firms' governance decisions are influenced not only by dyad-level characteristics but also by the characteristics of their IORs portfolio. Specifically, when the closest partners exhibit both cooperative and competitive dynamics, it impacts how the focal firm chooses to govern this set of relationships. To explore this level of analysis, we aggregated data from our respondents at the portfolio level, focusing on their most significant ties and considering firms that reported having at least two important relationships for innovation. We examined two portfolio features: relational embeddedness and trust. As previously discussed at the dyad level, relational embeddedness was assessed based on the

---

[3] We recognize the potential presence of reverse causality, suggesting that formal mechanisms may necessitate more frequent interactions. Nevertheless, existing literature (among the others, Dyer & Singh, 1998) supports our understanding of a strong relationship based on informal coordination mechanisms requiring frequent interactions, as opposed to weaker relationships reliant on formal mechanisms with less frequent interactions. We extend our gratitude to an anonymous reviewer for highlighting this aspect.

dimensions of length and strength. Trust, on the other hand, was evaluated using a 5-point Likert scale that asked respondents to rate the level of trustworthiness of their partners. However, in this case, our interest lies in understanding how portfolio features influence governance choices within individual dyads. To achieve this, we calculated the average values of length, strength, and trust at the portfolio level.

We propose examining the choice to use or not use formal and informal mechanisms by considering the characteristics of the portfolio in which each dyad is embedded. Table 4.2 reports the results of our analysis.

In terms of the utilization of formal and informal mechanisms, we observe a similar pattern of relational embeddedness at the portfolio level as seen at the dyad level. The more embedded the portfolio of relationships, the more the focal firm tends to rely on formal arrangements. Informal mechanisms are less prevalent in relationships of long duration but are more commonly employed when the relationship is characterized by greater strength. Trust also follows the same pattern, but even more prominently: when the focal firm's portfolio exhibits high levels of trust, there is a higher propensity to use formal mechanisms and a lower inclination towards informal mechanisms compared to portfolios with low levels of trust.

We interpret these findings within the context of the competitive dynamics faced by Italian automotive suppliers, which are characterized by intense competition due to the contraction of national production and the ongoing innovation challenge. We observe that as the relationship between partners becomes longer, there is a greater inclination to establish formal contracts, indicating a reduced perceived risk of exploitation.

Table 4.2 Portfolio's features and governance choices

		Informal mechanisms	*Formal mechanisms*
Portfolio's relational embeddedness	Long duration	2.33	3.71
	Short duration	2.21	3.51
	High strength	2.21	3.67
	Low strength	2.30	3.51
Portfolio's trust	High trust	2.12	3.71
	Low trust	2.40	3.48

Note The use of Formal and Informal Mechanisms are measured with a refined 5-point Likert scale ranging from 1 denoting negligible utilization to a rating of 5 indicating extensive and robust implementation

Conversely, when trust is still in the process of development between the parties, formal mechanisms are used less frequently due to their perceived higher risk, while informal mechanisms are more commonly employed.

4.5.3 *The Network Level of Analysis*

The network level, the third level of analysis discussed in Chapter 2, provides valuable insights into the governance choices of firms regarding their IORs. Two perspectives can be adopted at the network level: the whole-network perspective and the focal-firm perspective. Given the nature of the data in our database, which was not explicitly designed to represent the whole-network level, we focused on the focal-firm perspective. Specifically, we investigated three different measures that describe the structural position of firms within the overall network under analysis: betweenness centrality, in-degree centrality, and out-degree centrality. Each measure captures a slightly different concept and is measured in a distinct manner.

Betweenness centrality quantifies the degree to which a node lies on the shortest paths between two other nodes in the network. It captures the node's role as a bridge or bottleneck in facilitating interactions between other nodes. In-degree centrality, on the other hand, counts the number of incoming links to a node, for example indicating how frequently the node is cited by others as an important innovation partner. Similarly, out-degree centrality counts the number of outgoing links from a node, for example reflecting the number of other nodes that the focal firm identifies as its crucial innovation partners. These measures have distinct meanings and interpretations. Betweenness centrality highlights a node's potential brokerage opportunities within the network; in-degree and out-degree centrality, on the other hand, gauge a node's popularity, influence, or reach within the network, indicating its level of prominence or connectivity.

These measures serve as significant indicators of contextual factors that impact firms' governance choices, as extensively discussed in Chapter 2. Table 4.3 showcases the results of our analysis regarding the brokerage and centrality measures and their impact on firms' governance choices. Specifically, it examines the firms' decisions regarding the utilization of formal and informal mechanisms: in these analyses, the variables were dichotomized into high/low categories using the threshold determined by whether they were above or below their respective means.

Table 4.3 Focal-firm's features at the network level and governance choices

		Informal mechanisms	Formal mechanisms
Brokerage	High betweenness centrality	2.09	3.71
	Low betweenness centrality	2.33	3.57
Centrality	High in-degree centrality	2.08	3.68
	Low in-degree centrality	2.35	3.58
	High out-degree centrality	2.32	3.58
	Low out-degree centrality	2.22	3.63

Note The use of Formal and Informal Mechanisms are measured with a refined 5-point Likert scale ranging from 1 denoting negligible utilization to a rating of 5 indicating extensive and robust implementation

Consistent with existing literature, our findings support the notion that brokers, being influential actors in a network, tend to prefer formal governance mechanisms while utilizing fewer informal mechanisms. Similarly, the results reveal a similar pattern for firms with higher in-degree centrality, which signifies their popularity within the network. These firms exhibit a greater tendency to employ formal mechanisms and a lesser reliance on informal ones. Conversely, firms with higher out-degree centrality demonstrate a greater inclination toward informal mechanisms and a reduced utilization of formal mechanisms. These contrasting outcomes align with our expectations, as the two centrality measures reflect the power/dependence dichotomy discussed in Chapter 2, with in-degree representing the power dimension and out-degree representing the dependence dimension.

4.6 The Diffusion of Governance Choices

As outlined in Chapter 3, in addition to the contextual factors that influence exchange hazards and guide firms' governance choices for their IORs, firms also employ various approaches in making governance decisions. Factors such as learning processes, optimization, and evolution lead firms to identify "common governance practices".

Hence, apart from considering the variable that captures the level of formal and informal mechanisms adopted in the governance of IORs, we introduced an additional variable that holds particular significance for portfolio and network-level analysis: the replication of the use of formal and informal mechanisms. This replication variable captures the similarity of governance choices across the firm's most important ties within their IORs portfolio. For instance, if a focal firm consistently employs high levels of formal governance in all its significant ties, it will have a replication value close to 1. Conversely, if the firm utilizes varying levels of formality across different relationships, its replication value will be closer to 0 (Table 4.4).

Regarding the structural embeddedness explored at the portfolio level, we find that the length of the portfolio significantly impacts the choice to replicate formal mechanisms. Firms with portfolios consisting of shorter

Table 4.4 The diffusion of governance choice at the portfolio and network level

		Replication of use of informal mechanisms	Replication of use of formal mechanisms
Portfolio's relational embeddedness	Long duration	0.48	0.84
	Short duration	0.47	0.92
	High strength	0.51	0.83
	Low strength	0.44	0.82
Portfolio's trust	High trust	0.41	0.84
	Low trust	0.54	0.81
Brokerage	High betweenness centrality	0.45	0.85
	Low betweenness centrality	0.49	0.82
Centrality	High in-degree centrality	0.44	0.85
	Low in-degree centrality	0.49	0.82
	High out-degree centrality	0.48	0.83
	Low out-degree centrality	0.48	0.83

Note The Replication variable, measured on a scale from 0 to 1, signifies the extent of consistency in utilizing formal governance across significant ties; a replication value nearing 1 indicates a consistently high level, whereas a value nearing 0 suggests varied levels of formality across these relationships

relationships tend to replicate the use of formal mechanisms more than those with portfolios characterized by longer relationships. On the other hand, the strength of relationships within the portfolio particularly influences the decision to replicate the use of informal mechanisms. When the portfolio comprises strong relationships, the focal firm is more inclined to replicate informal mechanisms compared to portfolios with weaker relationships. These findings indicate that when the focal firm's most crucial relationships are well-established and of long duration, there is a tendency towards customizing formal arrangements. Simultaneously, there is a consistent utilization of informal mechanisms across these relationships. This behavior is associated with considerations of fairness and social identity, highlighting the importance of maintaining interpersonal relationships and fostering a sense of shared identity within the network.

Conversely, different levels of trust in portfolios are associated with varying degrees of replication for both formal and informal mechanisms. In portfolios with high levels of trust, there is a greater tendency to replicate formal mechanisms and a lower inclination to replicate informal mechanisms compared to portfolios with low trust levels. These findings are particularly significant in the context of innovation dynamics: when the focal firm operates within a network characterized by trustful and closely-knit relationships, it demonstrates a willingness to engage in binding contracts. This is due to the reduced risk of opportunistic behaviors, as transaction-specific investments are more secure. As a result, the firm is able to replicate its preference for formal governance mechanisms across its portfolio of IORs. Conversely, when trust levels are low, the firm cannot rely on the same informal governance approach with its partners. In order to build trust, it becomes necessary for the firm to differentiate its governance strategies among its partners, tailoring them to the specific needs and context of each relationship.

For what concerns the brokerage and centrality measures studied at the network level, we observed that high betweenness centrality has a significant influence on firms' governance choices, leading to an increase in the replication of formal mechanisms and a decrease in the replication of informal mechanisms. This pattern holds true when firms have greater brokerage opportunities within the network. Similarly, the in-degree centrality measure exhibits a similar trend, as it also reflects a firm's power and influence over its counterparts. Notably, the out-degree centrality measure does not have any noticeable effect on the replication of formal or informal mechanisms. These results suggest that when actors hold prominent and powerful positions within their network of business relationships, they tend to replicate the use of formal mechanisms without feeling the need for customization for different ties. Conversely, when a focal firm occupies a peripheral and less powerful position, it tends to adopt similar levels of informal governance with its counterparts. This approach provides reassurance and helps mitigate the potential risks of being exploited by partners.

4.7 Governance Choices and Firms' Performance

The final step in our analysis involves exploring the effects of governance choices on firms' performance. Given our focus on the EV technological transition and the role of IORs in navigating turbulent innovation contexts, we examine three key outcomes that hold particular significance: the focal firm's innovation, the exposure of the firm's product portfolio to the risks associated with the EV transition, and the firm's ability to develop new components specifically tailored to the EV market.

The innovation variable is captured by three distinct constructs. Firstly, Product or Process Innovation is represented as a dummy variable indicating whether the firm developed any new or significantly improved products or processes for its target market in the previous three years (coded as 1 for yes and 0 for no). Secondly, Product or Process Imitation as a dummy variable indicating whether the firm introduced new products or processes solely by imitating those previously introduced to the market by competitors (coded as 1 for yes and 0 for no). Lastly, Total Innovation and Imitation is a single dummy variable variable indicating whether the firm has engaged in either innovation or imitation (coded as 1 for either imitation or innovation, and 0 for otherwise). In our sample, 81% of dyads resulted in either imitation or innovation, 57% led to product or process innovation, and 44% to imitation.

The EV-risk variable has been constructed to assess the firm's exposure to the adverse effects of the EV transition in terms of its product portfolio. Each firm's product portfolio has been categorized based on the most relevant products, considering whether they will become obsolete with the new EV architecture, remain unaffected during the transition, or are entirely new and dedicated solely to EVs. If more than half of a firm's products are at risk of obsolescence due to the technological transition to electrification, the dummy variable takes the value 1; otherwise, it is

0. Overall, the firms at risk from the EV transition represent 17% of the dyads analyzed.

The last variable captures the firm's ability to develop new components for the emerging EV market, demonstrating how collaborative innovation activities have enabled them to navigate technological turbulence. This variable counts the number of components developed by the firm for the new EV market, ranging from 0 to a maximum of 2 products (out of the 4 most relevant products produced by the company). Across the entire sample, less than 2% of the total dyads resulted in the firm developing a new EV component.

Table 4.5 presents the results of the analysis examining the utilization of high/low levels of informal and formal governance (with the means used as the threshold) and their replication across the firms' most important ties, and their influence on the three performance variables described above.

The analysis results provide several insightful findings. In relationships governed with *low levels of informality*, we observe that they carry a lower risk associated with vehicle electrification as compared to high-informality relationships. However, they outperform in terms of innovation (both total and separate) and the development of new EV components. On the other hand, when firms choose *low levels of formality* in governing their IORs, they face higher risks associated with vehicle electrification compared to high-formality relationships. Furthermore, they underperform in terms of innovation (both total and separate) and the creation of new EV components.

Regarding the replication approach, when firms have *low levels of replication of informal mechanisms*, their collaborative relationships face lower risks associated with vehicle electrification compared to relationships with *high replication of informal mechanisms*. Moreover, they excel in terms of innovation (both total and separate) and the creation of new components. Similarly, when the replication of formal mechanisms is low, the dyad faces higher risks associated with vehicle electrification compared to relationships with high replication of formal mechanisms. Additionally, they underperform in terms of innovation (both total and separate) and the creation of new components.

These results suggest that informal mechanisms do not contribute to positive outcomes in terms of innovation performance and the ability to navigate turbulent technological times. Conversely, high levels of

Table 4.5 The performance effects of governance choices

		Innovation outcomes			EV-risk	New EV comp.
		Tot. Inn&Imit.	Innovation	Imitation		
Informal mechanisms	High Informal mechanisms	0.82	0.58	0.42	0.21	0.00
	Low Informal mechanisms	0.83	0.60	0.45	0.17	0.05
Formal mechanisms	High Formal mechanisms	0.85	0.61	0.45	0.18	0.04
	Low Formal mechanisms	0.77	0.53	0.41	0.19	0.01
Replication of Use of Informal mechanisms	High Replication Informal mechanisms	0.82	0.58	0.44	0.20	0.01
	Low Replication Informal mechanisms	0.83	0.60	0.43	0.18	0.06
Replication of Use of Formal Mechanisms	High Replication Formal mechanisms	0.85	0.61	0.45	0.18	0.04
	Low Replication Formal mechanisms	0.75	0.51	0.39	0.19	0.00

formality in the governance of IORs are associated with higher innovation performance and better ability to address the EV transition. Similar findings are observed at the portfolio level, where relationships with low replication of informal mechanisms generally yield good outcomes in terms of innovation, while hindering their ability to tackle technological challenges. However, low replication of formal mechanisms is detrimental to a firm's innovation performance and ability to address the EV transition.

In summary, when firms govern their collaborative innovation relationships in turbulent and uncertain technological times, utilizing formal mechanisms and diffusing this governance approach to their IORs portfolio is beneficial. On the other hand, high levels of informal mechanisms do not yield positive results for collaborative innovation, and firms that do not replicate their use achieve better outcomes in terms of technological challenges. This suggests that in turbulent and uncertain times, informal mechanisms should be used sparingly and customized with careful consideration for each collaborative innovation relationship.

4.8 Concluding Remarks

In this chapter, we have highlighted the criticality of the innovation challenge and the organization of innovation activities for Italian firms in successfully navigating the green transition. The unique characteristics of innovation management in the automotive industry underscore the importance for automotive suppliers to develop effective IORs, as their management plays a pivotal role in determining their success. In this regard, we utilized data on Italian automotive suppliers to address three main objectives: (i) investigating how contextual characteristics at the dyad, portfolio, and network levels influence firms' governance choices; (ii) examining how certain contextual factors impact organizational processes such as learning, optimization, and evolution effects, thereby influencing the adoption of common governance approaches among IORs; (iii) exploring how governance choices and the diffusion of governance approaches affect firms' outcomes in terms of collaborative innovation performance and their ability to navigate technological transitions.

Overall, our findings demonstrate that the decision to rely on formal and informal governance mechanisms is driven by both contextual relational features and firms' organizational practices, and these choices can either support or hinder firms' innovation outcomes. A notable insight arising from our results is that while informal mechanisms have traditionally been considered fundamental for collaborative innovation, their effectiveness may be diminished in contexts where technological uncertainty stemming from a paradigm shift is particularly high, and when the competitive dynamics within the industry are intense. Therefore, it becomes crucial for managers to delve into the intricacies of governance choices in IORs, particularly when the innovation challenge is paramount to a firm's survival.

References

Anderson, P., & Tushman, M. L. (1990). Technological discontinuities and dominant designs: A cyclical model of technological change. *Administrative Science Quarterly, 35*(4), 604–633.

Bastian, A., & Börjesson, M. (2015). Peak car? Drivers of the recent decline in Swedish car use. *Transport Policy, 42*, 94–102.

Calabrese, G. (2020). The Italian automotive industry: Between old and new development factors. In A. Covarrubias & S. M. Ramírez Perez (Eds.), *New frontiers of the automobile industry: Exploring Geographies, technology, and institutional challenges* (pp. 163–201). Springer International Publishing.

Calabrese, G., & Erbetta, F. (2004, 4–7 Aprile). *Outsourcing and firm performance: Evidence from Italian automotive suppliers.* Paper presented at the 13th Annual IPSERA Conference, Catania.

Clark, K. B., & Fujimoto, T. (1991). *Product development performance.* Harvard Business School Press.

Dillman, D. A. (2000). *Mail and internet surveys: The tailored design method* (Vol. 2). Wiley.

Dyer, J. H., & Singh, H. (1998). The relational view: Cooperative strategy and sources of interorganizational competitive advantage. *The Academy of Management Review, 23*(4), 660–679. http://www.jstor.org/stable/259056

Gulati, R., Nohria, N., & Zaheer, A. (2000). Strategic networks. *Strategic Management Journal, 21*(3), 199–201. https://doi.org/10.1002/(sici)1097-0266(200003)21:3%3C199::aid-smj98%3E3.0.co;2-0

Helper, S., MacDuffie, J., & Sabel, C. F. (2000). Pragmatic collaborations: Advancing knowledge while controlling opportunism. *Industrial and Corporate Change, 9*(3), 443–488.

Helper, S., & Sako, M. (1995). Supplier relations in Japan and the United States: Are they converging? *MIT Sloan Management Review, 36*(Spring), 77–84.

Helper, S., & Sako, M. (2010). Management innovation in supply chain: Appreciating Chandler in the twenty-first century. *Industrial and Corporate Change, 19*(2), 399–429. https://doi.org/10.1093/icc/dtq012

Jacobides, M. G., MacDuffie, J. P., & Tae, C. J. (2016). Agency, structure, and the dominance of OEMs: Change and stability in the automotive sector. *Strategic Management Journal, 37*(9), 1942–1967. https://doi.org/10.1002/smj.2426

Jean, R.-J.B., Sinkovics, R. R., & Hiebaum, T. P. (2014). The effects of supplier involvement and knowledge protection on product innovation in customer–supplier relationships: A study of global automotive suppliers in China. *Journal of Product Innovation Management, 31*(1), 98–113. https://doi.org/10.1111/jpim.12082

Lee, J., & Berente, N. (2012). Digital innovation and the division of innovative labor: Digital controls in the automotive industry. *Organization Science, 23*(5), 1428–1447. https://doi.org/10.1287/orsc.1110.0707

Metz, D. (2013). Peak car and beyond: The fourth era of travel. *Transport Reviews, 33*(3), 255–270.

Moretti, A. (2018). Le relazioni inter-organizzative come fattore di competitività. L'innovazione delle imprese automotive italiane. In A. Moretti & F. Zirpoli (Eds.), *Osservatorio sulla componentistica automotive italiana 2018* (Vol. 3, pp. 227–249). Edizioni Ca' Foscari—Digital Publishing.

Moretti, A., & Zirpoli, F. (2017a). L'innovazione delle imprese della componentistica automotive: risorse interne e relazioni tra imprese. *Sociologia del lavoro*.

Moretti, A., & Zirpoli, F. (2017b). L'innovazione e le relazioni inter-organizzative. In A. Moretti & F. Zirpoli (Eds.), *Osservatorio sulla componentistica automotive italiana 2017* (pp. 119–142). Edizioni Ca' Foscari—Digital Publishing.

Moretti, A., & Zirpoli, F. (2021a). Le collaborazioni inter-organizzative in un contesto in cambiamento. In A. Moretti & F. Zirpoli (Eds.), *Osservatorio sulla componentistica automotive italiana 2021* (pp. 215–228). Edizioni Ca' Foscari.

Moretti, A., & Zirpoli, F. (Eds.). (2021b). *Osservatorio sulla componentistica automotive italiana 2021* (Vol. 5). Edizioni Ca' Foscari.

Moretti, A., & Zirpoli, F. (2023). Sviluppo tecnologico e trasformazione dell'industria automotive italiana. In G. Calabrese, A. Moretti, & F. Zirpoli (Eds.), *Osservatorio sulle trasformazioni dell'ecosistema automotive italiano 2022* (pp. 45–52). Edizioni Ca' Foscari—Digital publishing.

Poppo, L., & Zenger, T. (2002). Do formal contracts and relational governance function as substitutes or complements? *Strategic Management Journal, 23*(8), 707–725. https://doi.org/10.1002/smj.249

Sabel, C. F. (1996). Learning by monitoring: The institutions of economic development. In N. Smelser & R. Swedberg (Eds.), *The Handbook of Economic Sociology* (pp. 137–165). Princeton University Press.

Sako, M. (2004). Supplier development at Honda, Nissan and Toyota: Comparative case studies of organizational capability enhancement. *Industrial and Corporate Change, 13*(2), 281–308. https://doi.org/10.1093/icc/dth012

Schulze, A., Paul MacDuffie, J., & Täube, F. A. (2015). Introduction: Knowledge generation and innovation diffusion in the global automotive industry—Change and stability during turbulent times. *Industrial and Corporate Change, 24*(3), 603–611. https://doi.org/10.1093/icc/dtv015

Takeishi, A. (2001). Bridging inter- and intra-firm boundaries: Management of supplier involvement in automobile product development. *Strategic Management Journal, 22*, 403–433.

Takeishi, A. (2002). Knowledge partitioning in the inter-firm division of labor: The case of automotive product development. *Organization Science, 13*, 321–338.

Whitford, J. (2005). *The new old economy. Networks, institutions, and the organizational transformation of american manufacturing.* Oxford University Press.

Whitford, J., & Enrietti, A. (2005). Surviving the fall of a king: The regional institutional implications of crisis at Fiat Auto. *International Journal of Urban and Regional Research, 29*(4), 771–795.

Whitford, J., & Zeitlin, J. (2004). Governing decentralized production: Institutions, public policy, and the prospects for inter-firm collaboration in US manufacturing. *Industry and Innovation, 11*(1–2), 11–44. https://doi.org/10.1080/1366271042000200439

Wittwer, R., Gerike, R., & Hubrich, S. (2019). Peak-car phenomenon revisited for urban areas: Microdata analysis of household travel surveys from five European capital cities. *Transportation Research Record, 2673*(3), 686–699.

Zirpoli, F. (2010). *Organizzare l'innovazione. Strategie di esternalizzazione e processi di apprendimento in Fiat Auto.* Il Mulino.

Zirpoli, F., & Becker, M. C. (2011a). The limits of design and engineering outsourcing: Performance integration and the unfulfilled promises of modularity. *R&D Management, 41*(1), 21–43.

Zirpoli, F., & Becker, M. C. (2011b). What happens when you outsource too much? *MIT Sloan Management Review, 52*, 59–64.

Zirpoli, F., & Caputo, M. (2002). The nature of buyer-supplier relationships in co-design activities: The Italian auto industry case. *International Journal of Operations & Production Management, 22*, 1389–1410.

CHAPTER 5

Governing IORs for Innovation in Times of Disruption

Abstract This book investigated the effective management of inter-organizational relationships (IORs) in innovation contexts characterized by high uncertainty. Two research questions are addressed: (1) How do relational and contractual mechanisms vary in value based on contextual factors? and (2) How do firms make effective governance decisions for their IORs from a dynamic perspective? Theoretical implications underscore the importance of considering the relational context and multiple layers of analysis to understand the effectiveness of governance mechanisms. Designing effective governance strategies in turbulent and uncertain environments necessitates the development of specific organizational capabilities for adapting to emerging challenges. Managerial implications emphasize the need for firms to cultivate relational capabilities and acquire competencies to navigate trade-offs and tensions across different levels of analysis. The case of the Italian Automotive Supply-chain allowed to highlight the significance of collaboration in the face of technological transformations.

Keywords Inter-organizational relationships · Governance mechanisms · Relational capabilities · Technological transformations · Automotive supply chain

© The Author(s), under exclusive license to Springer Nature Switzerland AG 2024
S. Li Pira and A. Moretti, *Governing Interorganizational Relationships for Innovation*,
https://doi.org/10.1007/978-3-031-50229-3_5

5.1 The Challenges of Governing IORs for Innovation in Times of Disruption

The book's primary focus was to understand the challenges faced by firms when managing IORs with various partners in environments characterized by change and uncertainty. As previous studies have highlighted, forming partnerships to effectively address future challenges through innovation is of key relevance. However, it remains unclear how the increased dynamism experienced by firms in turbulent times impacts the capability of these partnerships to produce innovation outcomes.

The significance of innovation performance for firms' competitiveness extends across various industrial sectors, making the study of interorganizational relationships a central focus in the field of strategy and organization studies. Scholars have explored several dimensions of collaborative inter-firm relations to better understand the circumstances under which firms can leverage external partners to achieve higher innovation outcomes. The discourse surrounding firms' choices in terms of innovation processes has been dominated by the concepts of open innovation (Chesbrough, 2003) and innovation networks (Pittaway et al., 2004). There is now widespread agreement on the importance of interorganizational collaboration in promoting innovation within companies and recognizing that external sources of innovation complement a firm's internal resources (De Propris, 2002; Freel & Harrison, 2006; Tomlinson, 2010). However, how firms define and adapt their collaborative strategies for innovation remains a complex and multifaceted problem that has not yet been fully explored.

In the domain of innovation, in fact, several factors contribute to the complexity of inter-firm exchanges: (i) the uncertainty surrounding innovative projects makes it impossible to define the objects/tasks to be exchanged beforehand, (ii) collaborative innovation often requires partners to share proprietary knowledge to some extent, and (iii) innovative projects involve costly investments and inherent risks. Nonetheless, external collaborations are vital for firms' innovation outcomes (Chesbrough, 2003), and firms' ability to design effective collaborative innovation strategies—such as selecting external partners, defining the terms of agreements, coordination mechanisms, and task allocation—and adapt them in such complex environments can be a source of competitive advantage (Prashant & Harbir, 2009; Zollo & Winter, 2002).

In this book, we specifically explored two main challenges associated with the governance of inter-organizational innovation within two areas of investigation. Firstly, we examined how contextual factors, particularly those related to the firms with whom a company collaborates, influence the level of uncertainty and the transaction-specific investments, and affect the relative effectiveness of contractual and relational governance. Secondly, we investigated how firms make decisions regarding the governance of their inter-organizational relationships by considering their organizational learning, optimization, and evolutionary dynamics.

In particular, the first challenge revolves around the issue of mitigating risks (Abdi & Aulakh, 2017; Oliver, 1990; Rindfleisch, 2000) when collaborating with other firms, involving complex dynamics of trust and opportunism. Every firm that engages in inter-organizational innovation relationships faces this challenge, and the search for the appropriate balance between contractual and relational governance mechanisms (Eckerd et al., 2022; Faems et al., 2008) unfolds at three different levels of analysis: the individual partnership (dyad), the portfolio of inter-organizational relationships, and the network level.

The second challenge explores how firms can effectively develop their governance strategies for inter-organizational innovation relationships. As the literature acknowledges (Capaldo & Messeni Petruzzelli et al., 2011; Dyer & Singh, 1998; Parmigiani et al., 2022), governing these relationships is a complex organizational capability that involves both internal and external processes. In the pursuit of effective management of these relationships, firms can adopt different approaches to their decision-making processes, including problem-solving (Nickerson & Zenger, 2004), experiential learning (Mayer & Argyres, 2004), evolutionary (Doz, 1996), and political approaches (Brattström & Faems, 2020).

To complete our theoretical exploration, we analysed the automotive industry as a compelling example. The sector, in fact, is currently undergoing a significant technological transformation, primarily driven by the increased adoption of electric and digital technologies. This shift has led to a profound reorganization of innovation activities and collaborations within original equipment manufacturers (OEMs) and their supply chains. The industry has experienced a reduction in the number of components in a typical car's bill of materials due to the transition from endothermic to electric drivetrains. However, this reduction is countered by an exponential growth of electric vehicle (EV) components and infrastructural services. Since powertrain systems have traditionally been within the domain of OEMs, suppliers need to reorganize their engineering and design choices to adapt to the new technological ecosystem. In the Italian context, the green transition coincides with a critical period of declining domestic demand for components, intensifying competition among firms. As a result, automotive suppliers are currently confronted with a technological change that brings both new business challenges and opportunities, requiring the development of new competencies. Innovation activities, especially those involving interorganizational collaborations, have become even more crucial in order to maintain competitiveness throughout this transition.

5.2 How Firms Mitigate the Risks of Inter-organizational Relationships? The Contingent Value of Governance Mechanisms

In this book, we conducted an in-depth exploration of how firms can effectively manage their inter-organizational relationships (IORs), which play a crucial role in navigating turbulent times of change and innovation. One of the main findings from our theoretical and empirical investigation pertains to the contingent value of different governance mechanisms, which has been extensively examined in prior research (Cao & Lumineau, 2015; Eckerd et al., 2022; Keller et al., 2021; Lumineau et al., 2021). However, previous studies have primarily focused on one level of analysis at a time, such as the dyad level, the IORs portfolio level, or the network level, limiting the understanding of the overall dynamics.

In fact, scholars have explored the varying effectiveness of relational and contractual governance mechanisms and their impact on performance, primarily concentrating on dyadic relationships (Cao & Lumineau, 2015). The Transaction-Cost Economics (TCE) approach has been frequently employed to examine exchange hazards (Abdi & Aulakh, 2017; Oliver, 1990; Rindfleisch, 2000), suggesting that in situations where exchange hazards are pronounced, relying solely on relational governance mechanisms can become challenging for partners (Abdi & Aulakh, 2017; Rindfleisch, 2000), and contractual arrangements may lose their effectiveness in terms of coordination and control functions (Malhotra & Lumineau, 2011; Reuer & Ariño, 2002). When contracts fail to mitigate exchange hazards, as is often the case in innovation contexts, relational governance becomes crucial for enhancing mutual safeguards against opportunistic behaviours. Thus, exchange hazards serve as key drivers behind governance theories (Gulati & Zajac, 1998), as discussed theoretically in Chapter 2.

In our exploration, we adopted this lens and the dichotomy between contractual and relational governance to examine the contingent value of governance choices, extending the theory beyond the usual dyadic level of analysis and delving more deeply into the portfolio and network levels. Our analysis revealed that exchange hazards, including uncertainty and transaction-specific investments, exhibit different intensities depending on the analytical level and the adopted perspective (focal-firm vs. alters). Moreover, the value of relational and contractual governance often becomes polarized between the focal-firm and alters when asymmetries are present. What may be advantageous for one party may not be preferable for the other. Furthermore, this contingency is further emphasized when transitioning from one level of analysis to another. What may be valuable at the individual firm level becomes less effective when considered at the portfolio level or in terms of network structure. This analysis partially unravelled the tensions and trade-offs that arise when firms define their governance strategies, particularly when embedded in dense networks of interrelationships.

When we turned to the empirical exploration of these issues, we found that in a context characterized by high uncertainty and intense competition, formal mechanisms of IORs governance are generally preferred over informal ones. However, depending on the level of analysis and the contingent features we examined, the value of both formal and informal mechanisms can change. A noteworthy finding is that informal governance mechanisms, typically associated with higher IORs performance in innovation settings, may not yield positive outcomes when firms are confronted with a technological paradigm shift and fierce competition.

5.3 How Firms Develop Their Governance Strategies? A Complex Organizational Capability

The present book goes beyond the static analysis of the contingent value of governance mechanisms and explores a dynamic perspective on firms' governance strategies. In times of disruption, firms need to be able to adapt, change, and redesign their governance arrangements to effectively harness the potential value of their IORs, which is crucial for maintaining competitiveness. While the complementarity between relational and contractual governance mechanisms has been extensively studied, less attention has been given to the interactive practices that facilitate their development. As a result, the dynamics that clarify the contingent value of these governance mechanisms remain elusive in the existing literature (Faems et al., 2008; Keller et al., 2021; Mayer & Argyres, 2004).

To push further our understanding of these issues, the present book delved into the evolutionary and adaptation dynamics of IORs governance mechanisms, to understand how firms design their strategies for inter-organizational collaboration. In fact, in times of disruption, firms face new and unexpected challenges—often technological ones in the innovation domain (Kogut & Zander, 1992; Parker & Ameen, 2018). Given that different problems require unique search processes, it is essential for firms to identify with whom to collaborate and how to collaborate—e.g., defining the suitable governance structure (Nickerson & Zenger, 2004). As an example, different innovation projects will require access to the partners' proprietary knowledge, as well as other types of resource pooling actions: in these contexts, collaborations impose interdependent constraints on governance decisions. However, turbulent times require fast reactions, and firms able to answer quickly to new challenges are better positioned in competitive terms (Cyert & March, 1963). Thus, firms rely on intra-organizational processes for decision-making also to exploit their capacity to quickly set up new collaborations or to adapt old ones to changing times and challenges. We posit that when firms need to take decisions about how to effectively sustain their collaborations for innovation, they resort to four different decision-making approaches: problem-solving (Nickerson & Zenger, 2004), experiential learning (Mayer & Argyres, 2004), evolutionary (Doz, 1996), and political (Brattström & Faems, 2020). Each of these perspectives, deeply explored in Chapter 3, contributes to explain the firms' strategy to replicate vs. developing ad-hoc governance strategies for their IORs. The "replication dilemma," as described by Winter and Szulanski (2001, p. 737), refers to the trade-off between the benefits of discovering new ad-hoc solutions (learning and adaptation) and the advantages of replicating established routines within a firm (precision and efficiency) (D'Adderio, 2014). Within the governance of IORs, firms can draw upon their prior experience in managing external partners, which contributes to the development of relational capabilities manifested as inter-firm relational routines. Alternatively, firms may opt to explore novel ad-hoc governance solutions to manage specific IORs or sets of IORs, adapting their governance approach based on specific circumstances.

When firms are facing turbulent times of (e.g., technological) change, replication strategies have distinct value because firms can leverage knowledge and insights and adapt their consolidated competencies to new emerging challenges. Nevertheless, although replication presents advantages (Haunschild & Miner, 1997), it is crucial to consider the contextual value and efficacy of various governance modes in different relationships. This consideration is necessary to prevent the restriction of adaptability and to ensure that firms remain prepared for change in innovation projects (Winter & Szulanski, 2001). Uncovering how adaptation and change dynamics can be faced through replication strategies empowers organizations to design and implement governance structures that align with their objectives, allowing them to effectively address challenges and uncertainties in interorganizational collaborations.

In our empirical exploration of the Italian automotive suppliers' collaborative innovation relationships, we explored how replication strategies are influenced by IORs contextual features and how they impact on relationships' outcomes. What emerged is that formal and informal governance mechanisms are differently apt to replication strategies, especially when considering contextual features. When the focal firm operates within a network characterized by trustworthy and closely-knit relationships, it demonstrates a willingness to enter binding contracts—thus relying on formal governance mechanisms. This is attributed to the reduced risk of opportunistic behaviors, as the security of transaction-specific investments is higher. Consequently, the firm can replicate its preference for formal governance mechanisms across its portfolio of IORs. In contrast, when trust levels are low, the firm cannot rely on the same informal governance approach with its partners. To establish trust, the firm must adopt differentiated governance strategies tailored to the specific needs and context of each relationship. Moreover, when the focal firm occupies prominent and influential positions within its collaborative innovation network, it often replicates the utilization of formal mechanisms without perceiving the necessity for customization across different ties. Conversely, when a focal firm holds a peripheral and less powerful position, it tends to adopt comparable levels of informal governance with its counterparts. This is probably due to a sense of reassurance, and it aids in mitigating the potential risks of being exploited by partners.

Moreover, when exploring the firms' performance outcomes associated with different replications strategies, we observe that relationships characterized by a low replication of informal mechanisms typically yield positive outcomes in terms of innovation, although hindering the firms' ability to address technological challenges. However, when there is a low replication of formal mechanisms, it adversely affects a firm's innovation performance and its ability to navigate the transition towards electric vehicle (EV) technologies.

The exploration of the evolution of governance mechanisms emphasized the importance of adaptation and learning as relationships encounter new challenges. Through the examination of this evolution, we uncovered how different governance mechanisms (formal vs. informal) express their contingent value also in their adaptation and change dynamics.

5.4 Concluding Remarks and Future Directions

In this book, our research aimed to address an overarching research question regarding the effective management of IORs in innovation contexts characterized by high uncertainty. To answer this question, we further articulated two specific research questions: (1) How do relational and contractual mechanisms change in value depending on contextual factors? and (2) How do firms make decisions to effectively govern their IORs from a dynamic perspective?

Our findings have important theoretical and empirical implications. The theoretical implications are twofold. First, we observe that the effectiveness of governance mechanism strategies depends on the relational context in which they are implemented. Our preliminary investigation suggests that exploring only the dyadic level of interaction is insufficient to fully understand the contingent value of different governance mechanisms. To comprehensively examine the complexities of governance choices and design effective governance strategies, it is crucial to consider multiple layers of analysis simultaneously, including the dyad, portfolio, and network levels.

Second, we emphasize that designing effective governance strategies is a highly complex and challenging process, particularly when firms face turbulent and uncertain environmental changes, such as technological transitions. Therefore, firms need to develop specific organizational capabilities that enable them to make informed decisions regarding whom to cooperate with and how to govern their IORs. In our exploration of the "replication dilemma" (Winter & Szulanski, 2001), we underscore that governance mechanisms demonstrate their contingent value within the process of change and adaptation undertaken by firms. Thus, understanding the effectiveness of governance mechanisms without considering how firms develop these complex competencies, such as analysing emerging challenges, identifying suitable partners, and establishing appropriate governance structures by leveraging internal knowledge for quick and prompt responses, is limited at best and potentially flawed.

Overall, our study highlights the need to consider the relational context and the development of organizational capabilities when examining the effectiveness of governance mechanisms in IORs.

Our findings have also significant managerial implications for companies, highlighting the need to develop relational capabilities to face the complexities arising from trade-offs and tensions across different levels of analysis. Firms must acquire specific competencies and knowledge to effectively manage the contingent value of relational and contractual governance at the dyad, portfolio, and whole network levels.

Our empirical investigation focused on the Italian Automotive Supply-chain as the setting. Although this specific context may be seen as a limitation, it offers valuable insights due to the automotive industry's exposure to technological transformation. Both original equipment manufacturers (OEMs) and their suppliers must rethink and reorganize their innovation activities. The industry's openness to external sources of innovation is now crucial, given the adoption of electric drivetrain as the new dominant design and the increasing presence of digital technologies in operations. Therefore, understanding how to build and manage effective collaboration strategies is a critical task for management, as collaborative innovation remains a key driver of competitive advantage in the automotive industry. These challenges necessitate the development of new competencies and the dynamic adaptation of governance mechanisms for inter-organizational relationships.

The Italian automotive supply chain serves as a valuable case study, providing a stress test for various theoretical perspectives on collaborative innovation strategies. The innovation ecosystem in this context is weak and fragile, with long-standing dominance by a single car manufacturer. Suppliers have traditionally adopted a passive approach to innovation, lacking significant expertise or distinctive competencies in the industry's recent technological revolutions: digital transformation and the green transition (electric vehicles).

Future research should extend investigations to other empirical settings characterized by technological change and innovation-intensive dynamics, to further enhance our understanding of these phenomena.

References

Abdi, M., & Aulakh, P. S. (2017). Locus of uncertainty and the relationship between contractual and relational governance in cross-border interfirm relationships. *Journal of Management, 43*(3), 771–803. https://doi.org/10.1177/0149206314541152

Brattström, A., & Faems, D. (2020). Interorganizational relationships as political battlefields: How fragmentation within organizations shapes relational dynamics between organizations. *Academy of Management Journal, 63*(5), 1591–1620. https://doi.org/10.5465/amj.2018.0038

Cao, Z., & Lumineau, F. (2015). Revisiting the interplay between contractual and relational governance: A qualitative and meta-analytic investigation. *Journal of Operations Management, 33*, 15–42.

Capaldo, A., & Messeni Petruzzelli, A. (2011). In search of alliance-level relational capabilities: Balancing innovation value creation and appropriability in R&D alliances. *Scandinavian Journal of Management, 27*(3), 273–286. https://doi.org/10.1016/j.scaman.2010.12.008

Chesbrough, H. (2003). *Open Innovation*. Free Press.

Cyert, R. M., & March, J. G. (1963). *A behavioral theory of the firm* (Vol. 66). Prentice Hall.

D'Adderio, L. (2014). The replication dilemma unravelled: How organizations enact multiple goals in routine transfer. *Organization Science, 25*(5), 1325–1350.

De Propris, L. (2002). Types of innovation and inter-firm co-operation. *Entrepreneurship & Regional Development, 14*(4), 337–353.

Doz, Y. L. (1996). The evolution of cooperation in strategic alliances: Initial conditions or learning processes? *Strategic Management Journal, 17*(S1), 55–83.

Dyer, J. H., & Singh, H. (1998). The relational view: Cooperative strategy and sources of interorganizational competitive advantage. *The Academy of Management Review, 23*(4), 660–679. http://www.jstor.org/stable/259056

Eckerd, S., Handley, S., & Lumineau, F. (2022). Trust violations in buyer–supplier relationships: Spillovers and the contingent role of governance structures. *Journal of Supply Chain Management, 58*(3), 47–70. https://doi.org/10.1111/jscm.12270

Faems, D., Janssens, M., Madhok, A., & Looy, B. V. (2008). Toward an integrative perspective on alliance governance: Connecting contract design, trust dynamics, and contract application. *Academy of Management Journal, 51*(6), 1053–1078. https://doi.org/10.5465/amj.2008.35732527

Freel, M. S., & Harrison, R. T. (2006). Innovation and cooperation in the small firm sector: Evidence from 'Northern Britain.' *Regional Studies, 40*(4), 289–305.

Gulati, R., & Zajac, E. J. (1998). Commentary on 'alliances and networks' by R. Gulati. *Strategic Management Journal, 19*(4), 319–321.

Haunschild, P. R., & Miner, A. S. (1997). Modes of interorganizational imitation: The effects of outcome salience and uncertainty. *Administrative Science Quarterly, 42*(3), 472–500.

Keller, A., Lumineau, F., Mellewigt, T., & Ariño, A. (2021). Alliance governance mechanisms in the face of disruption. *Organization Science, 32*(6), 1542–1570. https://doi.org/10.1287/orsc.2021.1437

Kogut, B., & Zander, U. (1992). Knowledge of the firm, combinative capabilities, and the replication of technology. *Organization Science, 3*(3), 383–397.

Lumineau, F., Wang, W., & Schilke, O. (2021). Blockchain governance—A new way of organizing collaborations? *Organization Science, 32*(2), 500–521. https://doi.org/10.1287/orsc.2020.1379

Malhotra, D., & Lumineau, F. (2011). Trust and collaboration in the aftermath of conflict: The effects of contract structure. *Academy of Management Journal, 54*(5), 981–998.

Mayer, K. J., & Argyres, N. S. (2004). Learning to contract: Evidence from the personal computer industry. *Organization Science, 15*(4), 394–410.

Nickerson, J. A., & Zenger, T. R. (2004). A knowledge-based theory of the firm—The problem-solving perspective. *Organization Science, 15*(6), 617–632.

Oliver, C. (1990). Determinants of interorganizational relationships: Integration and future directions. *Academy of Management Review, 15*(2), 241–265. https://doi.org/10.5465/amr.1990.4308156

Parker, H., & Ameen, K. (2018). The role of resilience capabilities in shaping how firms respond to disruptions. *Journal of Business Research, 88*, 535–541. https://doi.org/10.1016/j.jbusres.2017.12.022

Parmigiani, A., Irwin, J., & Lahneman, B. (2022). Building greener motorhomes: How dual-purpose technical and relational capabilities affect component and full product innovation. *Strategic Management Journal, 43*(6), 1110–1140. https://doi.org/10.1002/smj.3356

Pittaway, L., Robertson, M., Munir, K., Denyer, D., & Neely, A. (2004). Networking and innovation: A systematic review of the evidence. *International Journal of Management Reviews, 5–6*(3–4), 137–168. https://doi.org/10.1111/j.1460-8545.2004.00101.x

Prashant, K., & Harbir, S. (2009). Managing strategic alliances: What do we know now, and where do we go from here? *Academy of Management Perspectives, 23*(3), 45–62. https://doi.org/10.5465/amp.2009.43479263

Reuer, J. J., & Ariño, A. (2002). Contractual renegotiations in strategic alliances. *Journal of Management, 28*(1), 47–68.

Rindfleisch, A. (2000). Organizational trust and interfirm cooperation: An examination of horizontal versus vertical alliances. *Marketing Letters, 11*(1), 81–95. http://www.jstor.org/stable/40216560

Tomlinson, P. R. (2010). Co-operative ties and innovation: Some new evidence for UK manufacturing. *Research Policy, 39*(6), 762–775. https://doi.org/10.1016/j.respol.2010.02.010

Winter, S. G., & Szulanski, G. (2001). Replication as strategy. *Organization Science, 12*(6), 730–743. https://doi.org/10.1287/orsc.12.6.730.10084

Zollo, M., & Winter, S. G. (2002). Deliberate learning and the evolution of dynamic capabilities. *Organization Science, 13*(3), 339–351. http://www.jstor.org/stable/3086025

Index

A
Adaptation, 51
Adaptation dynamics, 102
Ad-hoc governance solutions, 103
Alliances, 2
Alliance web, 31
Automakers, 11
Automotive industry, 3, 72
Automotive production system, 73

B
Betweenness centrality, 85
Brokerage, 35, 88
Buyer–supplier relations, 12

C
Centrality, 88
Challenges, 98
Change, 98
Collaborative innovation, 98
Collaborative innovation strategies, 20
Collaborative know-how, 29
Competitiveness, 98, 102
Conflict, 28
Contractual governance, 101
Contractual governance mechanisms, 20
Cooperation, 8, 20, 50
Coopetition dynamics, 28
Coordination, 2, 20, 50
Cultural distance, 23

D
Density, 32
Disruption, 2
Disruptive innovation, 6
Dyad, 20
Dyadic level of analysis, 81
Dynamics of governance mechanisms, 6, 50

E
Ecosystem, 2, 76
Electric vehicles (EVs), 3, 79
Embeddedness, 31
Enforcement mechanisms, 5

European market, 75
Evolution, 51
Evolutionary, 102
Evolutionary approach, 52
Exchange hazards, 80
Experience, 29
Experiential learning approach, 52

F
Fiat Auto, 74
Fiat Chrysler Automobiles (FCA), 74
First-tier suppliers, 73
Focal-firm centrality, 34
Formal contracts, 3
Formal governance, 3

G
Governance mechanisms, 2
Green transition, 79

I
Incumbents, 76
In-degree centrality, 85
Informal governance, 3
Informal mechanisms, 3
Innovation performance, 98
Inter-firm relational routines, 103
Internal combustion engine, 76
Interorganizational relationships (IORs), 2, 3, 6, 7
Italian automotive industry, 75

L
Learning, 29
Level of codification, 4

M
Multiplexity, 25

N
National Observatory on the Transformations of the Automotive Ecosystem, 79
National Observatory Survey on Italian Automotive Suppliers, 78
Network level, 20, 88
New entrants, 76

O
Object of exchange, 26
Open innovation, 98
Original equipment manufacturers (OEMs), 72
Out-degree centrality, 85
Over-embeddedness, 83

P
Peak-car, 77
Phase-out, 77
Platforms, 76
Political approach, 52
Portfolio, 20
Portfolio level, 84, 87
Position along the supply-chain, 21
Power, 82
Power/Dependence, 23
Problem-solving approach, 52

R
Reciprocity, 9
Relational embeddedness, 24, 32, 82–84
Relational governance, 101
Relational governance mechanisms, 20
Relational norms, 3
Replication, 87
Replication dilemma, 59
Replication strategies, 60, 103

S

Second-tier suppliers, 74
Size, 22, 82
Small and medium-sized enterprises (SMEs), 75
Stellantis, 75
Strength of relationships, 32
Structural embeddedness, 32, 87
Structural holes, 33
Suppliers, 12
Supply chain position, 81
Survey, 79
Sustainable powertrains, 76
Synergies, 28

T

Technological discontinuities, 78
Technological disruption, 2, 13
Technological paradigm, 76
The Network level of analysis, 85
The portfolio level of analysis, 83
Third-tier suppliers, 74
Transaction cost economics, 2
Transaction-specific investments, 20
Trust, 9, 26, 83
Turbulence, 6
Turbulent waters, 13
Typology of Governance Mechanisms, 3

U

Uncertainty, 20, 98

V

Vertical supply network, 72

GPSR Compliance
The European Union's (EU) General Product Safety Regulation (GPSR) is a set of rules that requires consumer products to be safe and our obligations to ensure this.

If you have any concerns about our products, you can contact us on

ProductSafety@springernature.com

In case Publisher is established outside the EU, the EU authorized representative is:

Springer Nature Customer Service Center GmbH
Europaplatz 3
69115 Heidelberg, Germany

www.ingramcontent.com/pod-product-compliance
Ingram Content Group UK Ltd.
Pitfield, Milton Keynes, MK11 3LW, UK
UKHW022154230426
12049UKWH00004BA/93